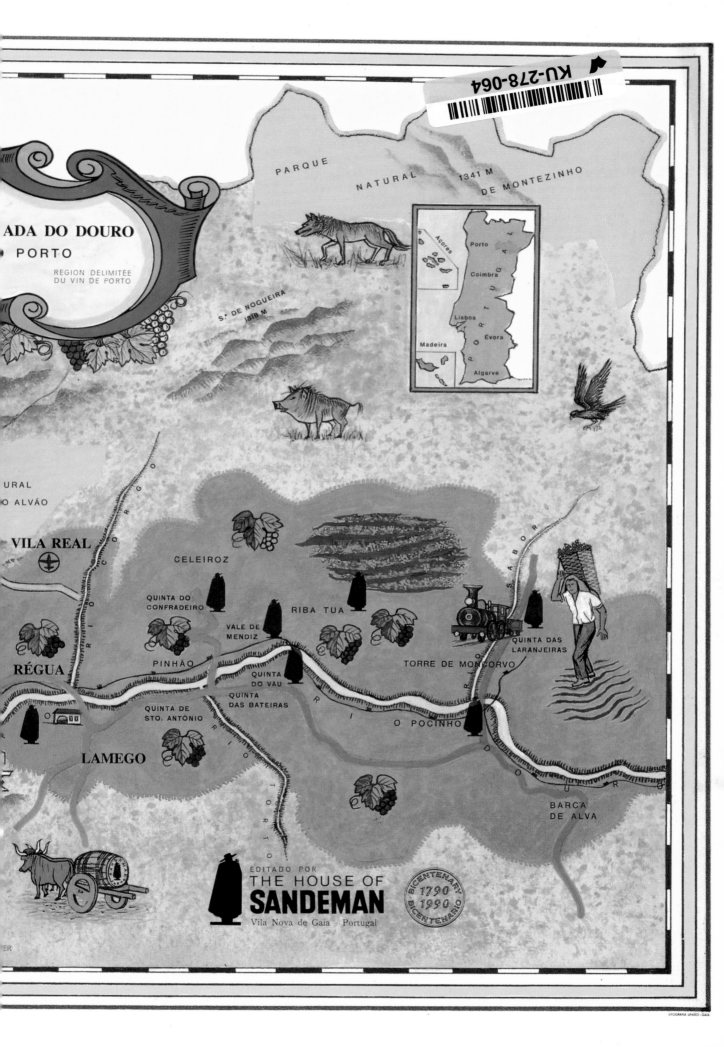

To Ken with fond memories
of the 1871 Port

Andrew Christmas 1991

SANDEMAN

Two Hundred Years of PORT and SHERRY

BICENTENARY · 1790 1990 · BICENTENARIO

SANDEMAN

Two Hundred Years of PORT and SHERRY

Ned Halley

GRANTA
EDITIONS

Sandeman: Two Hundred Years of Port and Sherry

© The House of Sandeman 1990

ISBN 0 906782 46 5

Published by
Granta Editions
47 Norfolk Street
Cambridge CB1 2LE

Granta Editions is an imprint of
The Book Concern Ltd

Designed by Dale Dawson

Design and production by
Book Production Consultants, 47 Norfolk Street,
Cambridge, in association with
Partnership Publishing, 23 Chilworth Mews,
London W2 3RG

Typeset by Cambridge Photosetting Services, Cambridge

Printed by Graficromo S.A., Cordoba, Spain

Contents

Acknowledgements

Special thanks for their indispensable help in preparing this book are due to the Sandeman family, and to the following: Marcus Clapham, Jon Jones, Jorge Mundt and Eduardo da Costa Seixas. Further thanks, too, for their invaluable assistance to John Bell, Gael Gonzalez, John Lockwood and Alastair Tower. All photographs and illustrations appearing in this book are the copyright of the House of Sandeman except for those on pages 5, 7 and 9, which are courtesy of *The Antique Collector*, and pages 96 and 136 by Ned Halley. Portraits on pages 13 and 15 kindly loaned by Alastair Tower. The illustrations of Sandeman properties and other subjects in Portugal (including that of the Sandeman quay at Vila Nova de Gaia on the front cover) are the work of William Prater, an employee of Sandeman in the latter part of the nineteenth century. The original drawings are on display at the Sandeman lodges. The illustration of the Watergate, Perth, is reproduced by kind permission of Perth Museum and Art Gallery.

Introduction

This book is a celebration of the two great wines of Portugal and Spain – port and sherry. It is the story of how these wines have come to be enjoyed worldwide, more so today than ever before, and the place that the House of Sandeman has in that long and colourful history. It begins with my ancestor's founding of the business in 1790 and reveals how Sandeman has become the world-renowned name that it is today.

Naturally we wish to boast about the care and craft that have gone into making our wines over the last two centuries. But here, too, is the story of how port and sherry have developed over the years, how their fortunes have fared in the face of changing fashions, tastes and opinions, even of politics and war. In the evolution of the wines and their accessibility to those who delight in them, Sandeman has played a central role throughout.

As Ned Halley tells this story, in his independent and resolutely non-technical style, it makes fascinating reading – providing much pleasure as well as enlightenment. As we toast our 1990 bicentenary, this book gives me fresh cause to raise my glass to our founder as we look forward to the *next* two hundred years of the House of Sandeman.

Chapter I

Beginnings

Even by the standards set by the great men of the eighteenth century, George Sandeman was remarkable for his spirit of enterprise. Self-doubt was not among his vices. As his third successor to the chairmanship of the company, Walter Albert Sandeman, once affectionately recalled: 'He was a man of small stature and, like many small people, held an excellent opinion of himself.'

Aged 25, young George founded the company in 1790 in the City of London. His expectations were scarcely modest. Writing to the sister, Jeanie, whom he had left behind in his native Perth that year, he had a firm riposte to her plea that he should return home.

> I shall remain where I am, till I shall have made a moderate fortune to retire with, which I expect will be in the course of nine years; which to be sure is a long time, but some lucky stroke may possibly reduce it to five or six.

So he wrote, on 14 May, six months before renting the wine cellar from which the business began – and clearly with an eye on the century's end as his deadline for commercial success. The confidence he expressed to his sister must have made her smile:

> It is but lately that I have taken up this project of growing rich, but I find it has been of infinite service to me already. One may see the marks of thriving in every line of my face. I eat like a man for a wager. People stand out of my way as they see me bustling along the streets. I have a good word to say to everybody I meet, and, as I am informed, I frequently laugh in my sleep.

The founding of the firm was very much a family affair. George proposed to start in partnership with his brother David (eight years his senior) running the business in Scotland. David clearly shared his brother's enthusiasm, and offered to put up the necessary capital.

But it was to his father, also George, a prosperous cabinet-maker, that the founder turned for initial finance – though not before he had already committed himself to buying his first stock. He had been encouraged into the risk by his brother's certainty that Father would provide. David had also hinted, it seems, that he would personally step into the breach if Father failed to oblige.

George made sensible use of his brother's support to put a little gentle pressure on his father. In the light of what he called 'my brother's assurance that I may depend on £300 at

The Watergate, Perth, from an early nineteenth-century drawing. George Sandeman was born at the family home in this fashionable thoroughfare in 1765.

1

The original of this portrait of David George Sandeman was painted by his friend Sir Henry Raeburn in 1814.

Christmas', he told George Snr in a letter of 29 November 1790: 'I have taken a wine vault and am engaged to put in that sum by that time.'

'I have, however,' he continued, 'some apprehension that in making me come under this engagement he means to advance me this money himself in case it should not suit you, which I was not before aware of, and although I could have no objection to being under the obligation to my brother, yet I should feel very disagreeable in taking a sum from him which he would otherwise employ to advantage in business of his own.'

Three hundred pounds was a modest enough sum with which to start a business. It is difficult to make comparisons with today's values, but in the 1790s, £300 would have paid about half the price of a new 'Georgian' terraced house in London. Looked at another way, it was ten times the annual earnings of a skilled labourer at the time.

David George Sandeman (1757–1835), the founder's elder brother, was described by Sir Walter Scott as a man 'with as intellectual a head as I ever witnessed'. He was a shrewd judge of good investments, and offered to provide his brother with start-up capital for the wine business in 1790. George preferred to borrow the necessary £300 from their father, but David did serve as a Sandeman partner, in Scotland, until 1796. The brothers separated this connection amicably, so David could concentrate on his highly distinguished career in banking and insurance – which included founding the Commercial Bank of Scotland.

George Sandeman's letter to his father of 29 November 1790: 'I have taken a Wine Vault . . .'. The letter is continued overleaf.

The reason George Sandeman wanted his capital by Christmas was, he told his father, 'that the wines must be laid in then, if it can't be done sooner, on account of the winter, and I need not observe that a man's credit here depends upon his punctuality to a day'.

Like so many brokers and merchants setting up in the City of London then, George was trading not from offices of his own, but in the coffee houses that proliferated in the Square Mile. Business was effected on a gentleman's word, and the trappings of smart premises were not considered, then, a *sine qua non* for the aspirant trader. (Insurance business had been successfully conducted at Edward Lloyd's Coffee House in Lombard Street for a century already, and dealers in shares continued to manage without a permanent Stock Exchange – motto: 'My Word Is My Bond' – until 1801.)

Sandeman chose to conduct his business from Tom's Coffee House in Birchin Lane, Cornhill. From the beginning, he appears to have specialised in the wines of the Iberian Peninsula. In 1792, the first year for which records survive, Sandeman sold 127½ butts of sherry in England and a further 25½ in Scotland – more than 100,000 bottles.

It was a propitious time to enter the port and sherry trade, as Sandeman was no doubt shrewdly aware. Portuguese and

A traditional irregularly shaped English bottle dated 1825. Also a brass corkscrew and brush, and a late nineteenth-century port bottle-stamp.

Spanish wines virtually monopolised the British market, and their quality had improved greatly during the century. The bottle shape universally used had just evolved to the conveniently stackable narrow cylinder – making it possible for the first time to lay bottled ports down in bins, and thus to create an interesting new style of wine: vintage port.

Characteristically, George Sandeman was not deterred by his inexperience in the trade from being the first merchant to ship a vintage port – the 1790, bottled in 1792 – under his own name.

Port shipments into Britain as a whole were now at an all-time high, reaching 50,000 pipes in 1792. The nation was in a mood to celebrate. London and the burgeoning towns of the provinces prospered hugely in the Industrial Revolution. There was even good news from Court. The mysterious illness that had struck down George III, apparently rendering him hopelessly insane, suddenly remitted in 1789. In a national outpouring of affection for the restored sovereign, the King's health was toasted as never before.

Britain was not renowned for its abstinence even in the gloomiest of times. The habits of some of the most eminent men of the day give an idea of the scale on which gentlemen then liked to take their wine. William Pitt ('the Younger'), Tory Prime Minister from 1783 to 1801, drank six pint bottles of port *daily* – a custom begun as a boy when wine was prescribed by his doctors for his weak constitution. Pitt's Whig opponents Charles James Fox and the dramatist Richard Sheridan were reputed to have similar thirsts.

Politics inevitably played an important part in the international business of shipping wine. With the outbreak of revolution in France in 1789, the supply of wines from across the Channel rapidly dried up. Shipments of claret, burgundy and the like were not to be restored for significant periods until after Waterloo, in Sandeman's 25th year.

Revolution and subsequently war with France were a mixed blessing to the British wine trade. How George Sandeman managed successfully to do business with Spain and Portugal in spite of naval warfare, the treachery of the Spanish government and, ultimately, the occupation of both countries is dealt with in the following chapters. It is enough to say at this stage that while Sandeman began his business with demand at an all-time peak, the supply side was similarly remarkable – for its potential perils.

Even at home, business did not always run smoothly. As a new name, Sandeman had to establish his clientele by the timeless method of travelling the country – with varying success. In the summer of 1793, George wrote to his father from Guisborough, Yorkshire:

I shall begin with dismissing the subject of business by informing you that my successes were very soon at an end and that I have had but very few orders since I left Leeds and Wakefield. My route since then (16 miles) has been almost entirely thro' a country till now 'terra incognita' to

Above: Early English wine bottles from the Sandeman Collection. Dating from between 1650 and 1722, they were made possible by the new glass-producing techniques of the day – and were prized possessions bearing the owners' seals.

Left: By 1765, the date of the earliest bottle in this group from the Sandeman Collection, the bulbous shape had evolved towards the cylindrical. It was this shape that made it possible to stack bottles in bins for long-term storage – allowing bottle-ageing and thus opening the way for single-vintage ports matured in glass rather than in cask. The bottle in the front row, second from right, bearing the seal of a coronet for Baron Clinton, Lord of the Bedchamber to George III, was made in 1790 and is the model for the special commemorative bottles produced for the Sandeman bicentenary in 1990.

Overleaf: English wine bottles, c. 1730–1784.

George Sandeman, the founder, at the age of 69, drawn by his son Edwin.

me where my object has chiefly been to see what business was done and whether it was accessible and worth my attention hereafter.

He spent more than a year on the road at this time, covering vast distances, and clearly undaunted by his disappointments. The same letter to his father continued:

By the time I reach York I shall scarcely have left one corner or recess unexplored in all this immense country nor in Northumberland, Durham, Cumberland, Westmorland, and Lancashire in all which making a large proportion of England there will not I think be above 2 or 3 Wine Merchants whom I shall not have called upon or satisfied myself about. I might add Nottingham and Derbyshire besides several other tracks.

George Sandeman, the founder.

He wrote to his father again in November:

I wrote you I think about 3 weeks ago or more from London. Since then I have had a pretty long tour, but hitherto almost unprofitable.

In that time, he had sailed from London to Bridport in Devon, on to Exeter and Plymouth, then Taunton, Wells and Bath in Somerset, to Bristol and thence 'to Warwick and perhaps Staffordshire and I hope to be in London within a fortnight'.

Disappointed though he may have been with the results of these epic journeys, made along the dismal roads of the day, at the pace of the horseback rider or mail coach, George acquired sufficient business to set himself up in his own London premises by the spring of 1794 – at 24 Old Jewry.

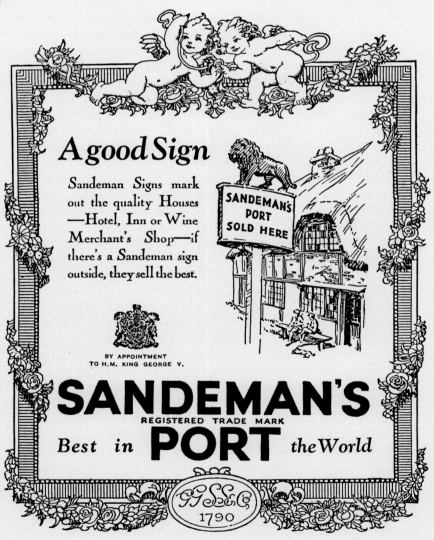

A good Sign

Sandeman Signs mark out the quality Houses —Hotel, Inn or Wine Merchant's Shop—if there's a Sandeman sign outside, they sell the best.

SANDEMAN'S PORT SOLD HERE

BY APPOINTMENT TO H.M. KING GEORGE V.

SANDEMAN'S
REGISTERED TRADE MARK
Best in PORT the World

GSSE&Co
1790

Chapter II

The Sandeman Family
Before 1790

George Sandeman, founder of the port and sherry house, was scion of a Scots family that has been traced back as far as one James Sandyman, who was serving as a lay preacher in the parish of Alyth, Perthshire, in 1567. It was here that the family became established, for in 1628 is recorded the marriage of John Sandeman of Alyth and Margaret Smith on 23 November of that year.

Their son, David Sandeman, in turn had a son, David, born on 13 April 1681. He settled in Perth – about 25 miles south-west of Alyth – in 1708, and appears to have begun the family's long mercantile history by entering the bleaching and textile trade.

David Jnr was twice married, first to Grizzel Eason who bore him four children, none surviving into adulthood. With his second wife, Margaret Ramsay, came happier times. They had 12 children – among them George, father of the founder of the wine business and Thomas, whose grandson was to succeed the founder as head of the company.

George and Thomas were the youngest of nine sons born to David and Margaret Sandeman. Eldest was Robert – one of many Sandemans who chose the Church – who was to have a famously controversial career as a clergyman.

Robert Sandeman's firm belief in the spiritual essence of Christianity rather than its career potential led him to join with the Rev. John Glas, whose 'Glasite' Church taught that established national churches – such as the Church of Scotland – had no basis in scripture. Robert married Glas's elder daughter Catherine, and became the leader of the sect, extending it from its 11 churches in Scotland to further outposts in Liverpool and London. He moved to London in 1760, where his preachings earned him considerable renown. By now, the sect was known in England not as the Glasites, but as the 'Sandemanians'.

Followers of Sandeman who had settled in New England persuaded him to join them there, and Robert sailed from Glasgow to Boston on 10 August 1764. He established several churches there, and was never to return to his native country. He died at Danbury, Connecticut, in 1771 aged 53, without heirs.

The simple faith that characterised Robert Sandeman's belief in a God-given rather than a man-made religion is summarised on his gravestone at Danbury: 'That the bare work of Jesus Christ without a deed or thought on the part of man, is sufficient to present the chief of sinners spotless before God.'

The Sandemanian churches were to continue attracting followers for more than a century. In London, leading elders of the sect included the great physicist Michael Faraday. But by

David Sandeman, born 1681, grandfather of the founder of the House of Sandeman.

THE HOUSE OF SANDEMAN

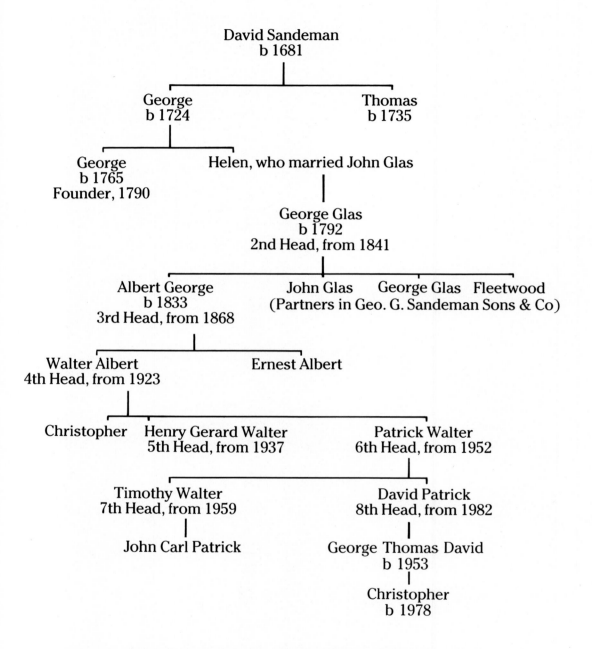

David Sandeman
b 1681

George
b 1724

Thomas
b 1735

George
b 1765
Founder, 1790

Helen, who married John Glas

George Glas
b 1792
2nd Head, from 1841

Albert George
b 1833
3rd Head, from 1868

John Glas   George Glas   Fleetwood
(Partners in Geo. G. Sandeman Sons & Co)

Walter Albert
4th Head, from 1923

Ernest Albert

Christopher   Henry Gerard Walter
5th Head, from 1937

Patrick Walter
6th Head, from 1952

Timothy Walter
7th Head, from 1959

David Patrick
8th Head, from 1982

John Carl Patrick

George Thomas David
b 1953

Christopher
b 1978

the end of the nineteenth century, the Sandemanians had faded on both sides of the Atlantic. As Walter Albert Sandeman was to recall, with a note of sadness, in his brief history of the family written in 1926: 'My uncle, the late Fleetwood Sandeman, visited Danbury in 1874, and as there were then only 27 members of the congregation he drew the conclusion that it would soon come to an end.'

Robert's immediate junior, second son of David and Margaret Sandeman, was David, born 1720. He earned a small place in Scottish history by the hazardous means of being taken hostage by Bonnie Prince Charlie in the Jacobite Rebellion of 1745. A magistrate of Perth, he was a political

George Sandeman's uncle, William Sandeman of Luncarty, was the first member of the family to record his Arms in the Public Register of all Arms and Bearings in Scotland, in 1780.

target when the Jacobite clans took over the city's government. Sandeman was taken south by the rebels on their march into England, but was released unharmed only a few miles out of Perth.

The next brother to reach adulthood was William, born 1722. He is known as William Sandeman of Luncarty – the name of the substantial estate he built up near Perth. He was the first member of the family to don the badge of the landed gentry – by recording his Arms in the Public Register of all Arms and Bearings in Scotland on 18 April 1780. He died in 1790, the year in which his immediate junior brother George provided the start-up capital for the wine business in London.

George, born in 1724, and his wife Jane had eight children, the sixth being the founder of the company, George Jnr. George Snr's eldest son, David George, was to become a partner in the House of Sandeman in its early years and his second youngest daughter, Helen, had an important part in the business, too.

George Snr's younger brother Thomas, like his brother the Reverend Robert, married a daughter of the Rev. John Glas, Anne Glas. Thomas and Anne had eight children, the fifth of them John Glas Sandeman. John Glas and Helen – his first cousin, as she was the daughter of his uncle George – married. It was their son, George Glas Sandeman, born in 1792, who was to become the second head of the House of Sandeman on the founder's death in 1841 – and from whom all subsequent heads of the company have since been directly descended.

Fleetwood Sandeman

Born in 1846, Fleetwood Sandeman was one of the original partners in Geo. G. Sandeman Sons & Co. He was also a keen sportsman, and is fondly remembered for his equally keen appreciation of the firm's manifold products. One enduring Fleetwood tale is of his travels in Ireland, from where a hotelier wrote to the partners in London begging them to persuade their brother to move on to another area as he was consuming the hotel's entire stock of old wine.

Fleetwood's sporting achievements bear rather closer examination. He was the founder and first captain of the Hayling Golf Club, the inaugural meeting of which was held at the Hayling Island home of his brother, Lieutenant-Colonel John Glas Sandeman, on 3 August 1883. His interest in salmon fishing lay behind his purchase of a farm at Gulla Gård in Norway, the story of which testifies to one of Fleetwood's many legendary kindnesses. He obtained a job on the farm for a Norwegian boy-sailor who was shoe-shining in London, having failed to get a passage home. The young man rose to become manager of the farm, and when Fleetwood Sandeman died in 1911 he left the property to him in his will.

Chapter III

Port Before 1790

In the story of port, 1790 is a landmark year. While George Sandeman was bustling about the business of becoming a City of London wine merchant, the British trade in Portugal was marking its largest annual export figure to date: 46,808 pipes – about 25 million litres – of port.

The British Factory, as the Oporto-based expatriate shippers were collectively known, could now celebrate their success in style, for 1790 also brought the completion of the splendid new Factory House. Its stern granite façade concealed elegant dining rooms and a grand, galleried ballroom which, as Charles Sellers wrote in his book *Oporto Old and New*, 'resounded daily and nightly to the festive carousals of men who were making for their posterity names to conjure with in the wine trade'.

The port trade had been centuries in the making. The first Englishmen to savour the delights of Portuguese wine were probably the doughty adventurers who took to putting into Lisbon and Oporto en route to the Crusades of the eleventh and twelfth centuries. Their intentions may have been to recuperate from the rigours of crossing the Bay of Biscay, but this did not prevent them from joining the Portuguese in their own struggle against occupying Moors. The promise of plunder – as close to most crusaders' hearts as the distant cause in Palestine – proved a powerful incentive. Thus did British soldiery establish some firm friendships with their hosts (they assisted immensely in sacking Moorish strongholds), and an equally solid thirst for the local wines.

Trade built up over the years, and by the 1600s, Red Portugal was as familiar as claret in England. The wine was not yet the fortified port we know today, but a red *vinho verde* from the Minho, north of the Douro. It was exchanged for the dried cod so prized in Portuguese cuisine (*bacalhao* as the fish is locally known traditionally appears in 1,001 recipes), shipped in from Newfoundland, and cloth from England.

Factors – overseas agents – of British mercantile firms were established in Lisbon, Oporto and Viana (at the mouth of the Minho) to facilitate trade. The factors in Oporto were particularly active in encouraging the farmers of the Douro to plant vineyards, and brought coopers over from England to teach local winemakers the art of making barrels. The quantity of wine available grew accordingly, but its quality remained doubtful. By 1700, Douro red wine was popularly known as 'blackstrap' – very dark in colour, raw and high in alcohol – and still unfortified. If there was any spirit included, it would be the few litres of brandy poured into the barrels just before shipment in the hope that this would prevent the wine spoiling along the way.

Ox carts brought the pipes of wine down tracks winding between the terraces for loading at the riverside.

The dramatic events of the new century's first years proved very fortuitous indeed for the Portuguese trade. The conflict sparked in 1701 by Louis XIV's claim on the Spanish throne for his grandson – and the consequent threat to Europe's balance of power – brought Britain and Portugal into a military alliance. In 1703, British ambassador John Methuen reinforced the pact by signing an important trade treaty in Lisbon. In exchange for Portugal's agreement to accept English woollens, Britain would reduce duties on Portuguese wines.

Duties on burgundy and claret had already been raised to punitive levels in retaliation against French foreign policy. Now, in the ten years of the War of the Spanish Succession that followed, the Methuen Treaty strangled France's wine trade with Britain as thoroughly as the Duke of Marlborough annihilated the Sun King's *grandes armées*.

Sales of Oporto wine – Douro wines for export – had been picking up even before the signing of the treaty. In the 1680s,

The spectacular valleys of the Alto Douro have been terraced since ancient times.

Overleaf: A timeless grape-treading scene in a Douro *lagar* – from a nineteenth-century painting in the Sandeman Collection.

the first years for which records exist, exports averaged 700 pipes annually. By 1715 the figure had risen to 8,000 pipes, and by 1749 it had reached 19,000. Oporto became the undisputed centre of the Portuguese wine trade as the British factors moved down from Viana, convinced of the superior quality of the Douro wines. The British grip on the trade tightened as the factors formed their own association in 1727, ostensibly to ensure high standards, but truly to form a purchasing monopoly in the face of rising prices from the growers.

Activity in the cultivable reaches of the Douro Valley was frantic. Much of the terracing that makes the river such an astounding spectacle today was first cut in the early boom days of two-and-a-half centuries ago. Fast as the farmers could work, however, they could not plant vines quick enough to satisfy the shippers' demands.

Inevitably, fraud crept in. Growers took to buying in cheaper wine from outside the region and passing it off as their own. To beef up such wines – or the thinner harvests of the Douro itself – it became common practice to add *baga* – elderberry juice. The shippers, ever anxious to satisfy demand from England, either turned a blind eye to such chicanery or indulged in it themselves. Quality suffered accordingly and the esteem in which Oporto wines were held by drinkers back in Britain – the only significant export market for the trade throughout the eighteenth century – plunged alarmingly and often.

The crunch came in 1755, when the shippers publicly proclaimed that the Douro farmers were adulterating the wine and overcharging for it. Whereas prices had previously reached as much as the equivalent of £10 a pipe, the British Association declared that the farmers would now be offered £2. Take it or leave it.

The farmers, facing ruin, turned to their national government in the shape of prime minister Sebastião José de Carvalho e Mello, soon to become Marquis of Pombal, whose antipathy to the British wine monopoly was by no means a closely guarded secret. Pombal's response to the growers' plea was to set up the Companhia Geral da Agricultura dos Vinhos do Alto Douro – the Alto Douro Wine Company. The farmers would henceforth sell all their wine to the company, which would in turn sell the wine to the shippers. The company would ensure that quality was always high, that the farmers were paid a fair price, and that the British Factory would in turn pay what the company considered a fair price, too. What was more, the company would select the wines suitable for export – they would have to come from grapes grown in a defined region of the Douro known as the 'Factory Zone' – and the British firms would be permitted to ship wines only to Britain.

While Pombal's concern was naturally to protect the good name of what had become one of his country's principal exports (his demarcation of approved vineyard zones in the Alto Douro pre-empted France's *appellation d'origine contrôlée* schemes by 180 years), he was also intent on ending the British monopoly over such a valuable national enterprise. To the protestations from the factory that his company would

The Spirit in the Wine

When was brandy first included in port?

History is, to say the very least, cloudy on this topic. The first dated anecdote is that of 1678, when the port trade was in its infancy. Two Liverpool wine merchants, the story goes, were despatched to the Douro to seek out wines to substitute for burgundy and claret following yet another breakdown in trade relations between Britain and France over Louis XIV's incipient warmongering. At Lamego, just south of today's important winemaking centre, Regua, the merchants called on the monastery, and were regaled by the abbot with a wine they had not previously encountered. Strong and sweet, the wine was – so the abbot reputedly confessed – the product of adding a good measure of brandy to the fermenting grape juice before all the fruit's natural sugar had been turned into alcohol.

The merchants duly bought as much of this nectar as they could afford and shipped it home. The consignment did not, regrettably, launch the era of fortified port. As late as 1754, as George Robertson points out in his book *Port*, shippers were complaining of a Douro grower who 'is in the habit of checking the fermentation of the wines too soon, by putting brandy into them while still fermenting; a practice which must be considered DIABOLICAL'.

Brandy, it had long been believed, should be added after fermentation to stabilise and strengthen the wine – in much the same way as elderberry juice was added to darken and flavour it.

Pombal's Alto Douro Wine Company changed everything. It monopolised not only Douro wine, but brandy, too, applying strict quality standards to both. And it forbade the addition of elderberry juice to the wine. The entire vineyard zone was cleared of elder trees, and their cultivation outlawed.

Pombal's new standards meant not only better wine, but improved prosperity for the growers, who were now able to invest in experimenting with new winemaking techniques. It seems likely, therefore, that today's port method must date from this time, even though it was clearly not in universal use until well into the last century.

That method is, in brief, that 110 litres of *aguardente* ('firewater' – colourless brandy from grapes grown in Portugal, made to 77 per cent alcohol) are added per 440 litres of fermenting must (grape juice). The brandy thus accounts for a fifth of the volume of the made wine.

bankrupt them, Pombal calmly retorted that if the British were unable to make a success of the port trade under the new regime, he had no doubt that the Portuguese Crown would be glad to assume the reins.

Their bluff called, the shippers could only pass the greatly increased prices on to their customers in England – with no consequent decline in demand. Quality clearly benefited from the newly imposed standards, and in the years until Pombal's fall from political grace in 1777, exports moved to a steady annual average of 20,000 pipes. Port, the first wine to bear a recognised guarantee of origin and quality, now won for itself the reputation of respectability that earned it the name of 'the Englishman's wine'.

The factory, in truth, had the best of both worlds. On the one hand the shippers benefited much from the improved quality of wine brought about by Pombal's rigorous enforcement of the new rules and the resulting improvement in port's renown. On the other, the shippers continued to bend the rules, buying wine from outside the Alto (Upper) Douro Factory Zone at cut price, adding brandy and elderberry juice as of old and

Oporto in the 1790s – as George
Sandeman would have seen it on his
first visit.

otherwise compensating for the disadvantages of having to deal with a tyrannical state monopoly by any means they could divine.

The relationship between the company and the factory settled down to one of mutual, if wary, respect. Both parties shared the objective of producing reputable wine at attractive prices. The British could boast that they had been the creators of the port trade, but they knew not to push their luck too far with their Portuguese hosts – who, in their turn, valued their good relations with Britain as a nation and its Oporto enclave for its mercantile endeavour.

This was the Oporto that awaited George Sandeman, a community summarised by the travel writer Rose Macaulay in her delightful book *They Went to Portugal*:

> By the 1780s, the shippers of Oporto were a cheerful, hospitable, quarrelsome, jovial and opulent society, closely intermarried and connected, living on excellent terms with their Portuguese neighbours and rivals, in the main patriotically British, protestant and loyal.

------------ **Chapter IV** ------------

Sherry Before 1790

It was the Moors, Muslim conquerors from North Africa, who gave sherry its name. They landed in southern Spain in the year 711, establishing an empire that within a decade covered more than half of the country. Seris was among their first settlements, close to the site of a terrible battle at Guadalete in which the Moors routed their predecessors, the Goths. Until 1264, Seris remained a Moorish stronghold and a prosperous agricultural and trading centre, surrounded by famously productive orchards and vineyards. Then came the avenging armies of Castile, reclaiming Seris for Christendom and adapting its name into the Spanish Jerez of today.

It is from Jerez (pronounced herr-eth in Spanish) that the English word Sherry – a partial reversion to the Moorish original – derives. And the wine owes more than its name to the Moors. Forbidden though alcohol was to them, the Muslims who held sway for those five centuries in Andalusia grew accustomed to enjoying the fruits of vineyards planted long before the prohibitions made by the Koran. The wine business in Seris, while officially outlawed, was allowed to carry on in the hands of the Christians and Jews (to whom the Moors allowed complete freedom to worship as well as to trade – a tolerance not reciprocated when the tables were turned). It is a pleasing paradox that an excise duty was levied on wine sales.

The liberation of Jerez was a victory for Spain, but by no means the end of their war with the heretics she knew as the Moriscos. Andalusia remained a battleground for another 200 years, with Jerez frequently at the centre of the action. The town's full name became Jerez de la Frontera in 1380 in an acknowledgement to its people that they stood at the very frontier between the Christian and the Muslim worlds.

War or no war, however, the end of occupation brought new life to the vineyards. King Alphonso X, a keen proponent of Andalusian wine, made gifts of the newly repossessed lands to his most loyal supporters, and encouraged new plantings. By the middle of the next century, wine exports, notably to England, were under way.

In the 1380s, Geoffrey Chaucer was writing about the strong – and probably brandy-fortified – white wines of Andalusia then used to beef up the flavour and alcoholic strength of those from Bordeaux, at that time an English possession. But it was a century later, with the final expulsion of the Moriscos, the end of war and the resumption of normal trade by sea, that sherry truly embarked on its golden age.

To promote exports, the local governor, the Duke of Medina Sidonia cancelled all taxes on shipments out of the ports serving Jerez, namely Cadiz, Puerto de Santa Maria and

The Palomino grape has for centuries been the predominant variety used in sherry-making – today more so than ever.

Sanlucar de Barrameda, in 1491. His proclamation referred to wines made specifically for the cool-climate markets of the north and known as *vinos de romania* – dark, sweet, fortified wines made as they were in ancient Roman times. Entirely different from the pale, dry wines preferred in the heat of Andalusia, these 'Rumneys' as they were known to the British merchants, were warmly appreciated in their chilly homeland. So quickly did the trade build up that the merchants established themselves in Jerez and the ports – encouraged by considerable incentives offered by Medina Sidonia. They were given houses and storage facilities, port privileges, even the right to bear arms. The Duke's magnanimity, which extended to offering the British his personal protection, was not entirely rooted in anglophilia. Expelling its entire Jewish population – 150,000 people – in the 1490s had deprived Spain of a large section of its mercantile class. Fresh entrepreneurial blood was now urgently needed to enliven the economy of the powerful new nation created by the union of its two kingdoms, Aragon and Castile – a nation whose sense of merchant adventure set Christopher Columbus forth, from the sherry port of Sanlucar, on his voyage of discovery to America in 1493.

The sixteenth century saw Spain emerge as a world power, and England likewise. Continually, the two nations stepped up their trading relations and rivalled each other on the high seas – often to the point of piracy. Throughout, the sherry trade boomed. Sack, the nickname given to the wine after the Spanish *saca*, a term used for any wine of export quality, was to become by the end of the century what writer H. Warner Allen said was 'for the English wine-drinker almost the one and only wine'.

At the beginning of the century, Henry VIII's marriage to Catherine of Aragon presaged good things for the sack trade. The subsequent divorce and the King's excommunication did bring difficulties for the English merchants in the sherry towns – not the least of which were the attentions of the Inquisition – but shipments continued more or less uninterrupted. By the time Elizabeth I came to the throne in 1558, annual imports had reached 40,000 butts (each of 500 litres), accounting for two-thirds of the region's total export production.

When the underlying hostility between Tudor England and Spain escalated from the skirmishes at sea, in which English 'privateers' attacked Spanish galleons, into a state of open war in the 1580s, the sherry trade found itself very much in the front line. The most celebrated incident was the raid on Cadiz of 1587 in which Sir Francis Drake 'singed the King of Spain's beard'. Drake's mission was to destroy the Armada being

Sandeman's vineyards at Jerez are typical of those that have flourished here for more than a thousand years.

Strong Wine, Fulsome Praise

Sherry appears to have been a fortified wine from its earliest days. The spirit used for the purpose was an invention of the Moors, who discovered the principles of distillation and gave the Arabic word alcohol to our language. The earliest sherry makers, given that Jerez was under Moorish occupation from 711 to 1264, would thus have had ready supplies of brandy.

As to the taste of the wine, it was almost certainly sweet, dark in colour and high in alcohol when produced for export. The countless literary allusions made to the wine by enthusiastic writers from Chaucer (1340–1400) onwards provide the best clues to its characteristics. The most famous write-up of them all came from William Shakespeare, who put his own adulatory words of praise for sherry into the mouth of the jovial Sir John Falstaff:

A good sherris-sack hath a twofold operation in it. It ascends me into the brain; dries me there all the foolish and dull and crudy vapours which environ it; makes it apprehensive, quick, forgetive, full of nimble, fiery and delectable shapes; which delivered o'er to the voice – the tongue – which is the birth, becomes excellent wit. The second property of your excellent sherris is, – the warming of the blood; which, before cold and settled, left the liver white and pale, which is the badge of pusillanimity and cowardice: but the sherris warms it, and makes it course from the inwards to the parts extreme: it illumineth the face; which as a beacon gives warning to all the rest of this little kingdom, man, to arm; and then the vital commoners and inland petty spirits muster me all to their captain, the heart, who, great and puffed up with this retinue, doth any deed of courage; and this valour comes of sherris . . . If I had a thousand sons, the first human principle I would teach them should be, to forswear thin potations, and to addict themselves to Sack.

prepared at Cadiz for the invasion of England. This he did with his customary despatch, blasting his way into the port with a squadron of 24 naval vessels, boarding 32 enemy warships in various states of completion, stripping them of every valuable in sight, then burning all but those in which he carried home the mountainous booty.

Incredibly, Drake remained three days in the great dockyard, finding time in the midst of this epic naval action to loot the huge quantity of sack that happened to be waiting on the quayside – 2,900 butts in all. The loss of this cargo is said to have been, on balance, of long-term benefit to the sherry trade, because its triumphal arrival in England popularised the wine there as never before.

The risks that Drake and his men undoubtedly ran to load up

such a great number of casks right under the King of Spain's nose give some idea of just how much the wine.was valued. Some historians do indeed say that it was the English love of wine, a commodity that had to be imported through what were almost invariably hostile waters, that motivated Britain's maritime build-up of the sixteenth century, bringing to the nation the sea power that was, ultimately, the key to Empire.

The 1600s brought peace, and continued prosperity for sherry, interrupted by Cromwell's Commonwealth (Puritans disdained such indulgences) which imposed high excise duties and made war on Spain in the 1650s. As they had done in Elizabethan times, the Spanish retaliated against attacks on their shipping by imprisoning English merchants in the sherry towns and confiscating their property, ships and stocks of wine.

Trade nevertheless revived with the Restoration in 1660. Samuel Pepys recorded his purchase of an entire hogshead (about 225 litres) of sherry in 1662 – 'the first great quantity of wine that I ever bought'. Twenty years later, Pepys visited the sherry country, and reported finding the British merchants in prosperous good order.

But hard times lay ahead. The eighteenth century began with resumed hostilities between Britain and Spain, breaking out into the War of the Spanish Succession in 1702. The Methuen Treaty of the following year granted preferential duty rates to Portuguese wines shipped from Oporto, 500 miles less sailing distance from England. This, and the extraordinary decision by the Cadiz authorities to impose new taxes on the export of wine, conspired to ruin the trade. British importers looked elsewhere for supplies, and found themselves well suited with rich wines from along the coast at Malaga, and from farther afield at Madeira. By the 1750s, the number of British merchants in Andalusia had dwindled to a handful.

The latter decades of the century brought gradual improvements to a trade that had at no time lost its reputation for good quality wine. Sherry (the name sack died out early in the 1700s) was still highly regarded by those who could afford it, and the trade continued to attract foreign entrepreneurs to Jerez. It was the generation of merchants who settled there in the late 1700s that laid the foundations of the modern sherry trade. It included Scots such as James Duff and C. P. Gordon, and the French émigrés Lacoste and Pemartin. With these new adventurers another newcomer, George Sandeman, was soon doing business.

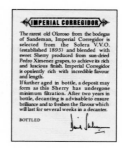

Chapter V

Wine, and War

For most of its first 25 years, George Sandeman & Co. was trading amidst major European wars. Hostilities to the Revolution brought France into conflict with every one of her neighbours, and by the summer of 1793 – the year Louis XVI went to the guillotine – Britain, Spain and Portugal were all at war with the new Republic.

Port and sherry sales were to benefit considerably from the consequent disappearance of French wines from merchants' lists, but George Sandeman regretted the war none the less. 'To see [the allies] cutting the throats of the poor French while the French are to cut theirs in order to prevent them embracing the doctrines of liberty and equality is insulting common sense,' he wrote to his father in August 1793, 'and I really fear from the manner people begin to talk that if this wanton bloody work continues much longer the common sense of the nation will rise against a minister or ministers who abuse the confidence and power put into their hands to create such calamities.'

Sandeman was clearly not a supporter of prime minister William Pitt's policy of war against the Revolution. The fact that Britain's role in the last years of the eighteenth century turned out to be one of the most disastrous episodes in Britain's entire military history somewhat vindicates young Sandeman's views, giving poignancy to the words he passionately expressed to his father:

> To think of the number of our soldiers lately slaughtered and to be, and the many widows and orphans brought to that situation by the wilfulness of one man one is tempted to cry out with the poet –
>
> > Oh! but man proud man!
> > Dressed up in a little brief authority
> > Will do such deeds before high heaven
> > As make the angels weep.*

This letter of 1793 gives a good impression not just of Sandeman's humanity, but of his shrewdness, for he accurately predicts the coming course of the war.

> I shall not be surprised to see them [the French revolutionaries] by and bye turn like Lions upon the Tygers and Vultures that are pursuing them. Our allies and ourselves may yet pay dear for our presumption and folly.

*William Shakespeare, *Measure for Measure* (slightly misquoted).

While the war on land was consistently mismanaged by the allies, allowing France successfully to overcome foreign invasions as well as her own counter-revolutionaries, sea power remained an allied monopoly. Toulon, France's premier naval port, was recaptured by the Republic late in 1793 from royalist forces, but not before the British navy – invited in by the royalists – had destroyed every ship in the harbour, accounting for the entire French fleet.

Patriotic thirsts in Britain could now be slaked with uninterrupted supplies of port and sherry from allied Portugal and Spain. The loss of French wine need not be mourned as the Englishman raised his glass to Jonathan Swift's adage from the wartime days that had begun the century:

> Be sometimes to your country true,
> Have once the public good in view.
> Bravely despise Champagne at Court
> And choose to dine at home with Port.

In 1798, shipments from Oporto reached a record that was not to be matched until the 1880s – 64,402 pipes. Sandeman, having started out as agents in London and Perth for the Oporto firm of Campion Offley Hesketh & Co., had since taken up with Warre & Co. Early letters spoke of the port ships being escorted by naval vessels – a precaution no doubt obviated by the destruction of the French fleet.

While Sandeman & Co. was certainly selling sherry as early as 1792, it was not until four years later that the firm was appointed agent to an individual shipper. This was James Duff of Cadiz, whose wines Sandeman first offered in a circular dated 1 March 1796. Customers could choose from no less than eight different sherries, ranging from 'Young Wine' (from the new vintage) at £17 per butt on board at Cadiz to 10-year-old at £25 10s and 'Superior Old' at £27. Freight and insurance were charged at £6 per butt.

According to Rupert Croft-Cooke in his book *Sherry* (published 1955), George Sandeman came to the Peninsula in 1790, 'and during the next two years he visited the wine-growing areas of Spain and Portugal before deciding that Port and Sherry were the two wines he could deal in.' From the available records, however, it seems likely that the founder's first such journey was made in 1796, taking in north Africa along the way. On 29 July, from San Sebastian on Spain's northern coast where he was staying with his friend and travelling companion Don Antonio de Tastet, he wrote home to Perth:

> My last I believe was wrote from Tetuan, from whence I returned to Gibraltar and by land to Cadiz. With much regret I left that city towards the end of April and after 12 days' journey arrived in Madrid, where I waited till beginning of this month for Tastet, who had remained behind at Cadiz, and we made this last journey together in a small chaise of his own in 10 days by way of Valladolid, Burgos and Vitoria.

I have been a good deal gratified with this opportunity of seeing the interior of Spain, having travelled just from one extremity to the other, from Gibraltar the southernmost point to this place at the foot of the Pyrenees which divide us from France, only 15 miles distant.

From the Castle we see the coast as far as Bayonne. All this part of Spain you will recollect was last year in the hands of the French, who had a garrison in this city, and would soon have had another in Madrid if a peace had not been hastily concluded.

Here as well as in several towns, where we stopt, it is surprising to hear the accounts they give of the good conduct of the French soldiers, who, without shoes or stockings and sometimes without bread, abstained from touching anything belonging to the inhabitants, who lived all the time, 14 months, in perfect security. The French General lodged in this house. I anxiously wish we were once more at peace with that people. If not brought about soon it is not doubted here that we shall soon be the only nation at war with them; and much apprehension is also entertained that Spain will be engaged in it on one side or the other; in the one case I should have to quit San Sebastian as the French would probably soon make their appearance, and in the other I should be obliged with all British subjects to leave Spain or retire inland.

As he wrote, Spain was indeed in negotiations with France – slyly agreeing with Napoleon Bonaparte to cooperate in the occupation of Britain's ally, Portugal. Spain declared war on Britain in October of that year.

The years that followed were, not unnaturally, difficult ones for the port and sherry trade. Britain and Spain engaged in a series of epic naval encounters starting with the battle off Cape St Vincent, Portugal's south-westernmost point, in 1797 – in which Horatio Nelson routed the enemy, and set the pattern of the sea war that was to keep mercantile shipping on the move. Not that there were no setbacks. The Royal Navy was all but crippled by several serious mutinies in 1797, and was at war with French fleets, too, both in the Mediterranean and the North Sea.

Undeterred, George Sandeman published a circular in January 1798 offering James Duff's sherries, on board at Cadiz, at prices no higher than those listed before the outbreak of war two years earlier. Hostilities in those pragmatic days, it seems, were insufficient grounds for the cessation of commercial relations.

In 1801, however, the port trade suffered a major setback. The Spanish staged a surprise invasion and forced Portugal to break with Britain. Lisbon and Oporto were closed to the Royal Navy. In that year, port shipments fell to 21,000 pipes from the 1800 figure of 56,000 – a level not again achieved until the last decades of the new century.

For George Sandeman, there was consolation in the Treaty of Amiens in 1802, the 'frail and deceptive truce' between Britain and France that was to last just 14 months, but that did allow the intrepid traveller the chance to see Paris and the wine country for himself. He took with him introductions to a number of producers, including the oldest Cognac firm, Augier Frères (although it was for Hennessys, in the end, that Sandemans became Irish agents). His main interest seems to have been Bordeaux, from where he wrote to his father in July – a letter now lost, but which elicited this reply from George Snr, marvelling at 'days where you walked many miles through rich vineyards seeing the various preparations for the vintage, wine presses etc, for the very best of wines viz: fine rich claret, being by far the best of all wines and which the late Dr Jas. Smith used often to say was the best for the Blood – Yea, Yea, he said it was both meat and drink and made one chearfull and in spirits in the morning and further if one was perplexed or vext it would make all without one smooth as velvet.'

Father and son were clearly of like mind when it came to claret, as the Sandemans were soon listing it on their circulars to customers. One dated April 1809 lists claret at £88 a hogshead (about 225 litres), compared to port at £95 per 138 gallons (627 litres). The very high relative price for the French wine reflects the scarcity of supply due to the war, and punitive rates of duty. Nevertheless, it was at this time that Sandeman established a connection with one of Bordeaux's great merchant houses, Barton & Guestier (founded in 1725). Sandeman later became London agents for the firm, and represented it in Britain throughout the remainder of the nineteenth century. The similar connection with Hennessy in Cognac, also dating from the early 1800s, continued in Ireland until the 1960s.

From the beginning, however, wines from Portugal and Spain were at the heart of Sandeman's business. Port, madeira and sherry – plus a variety of other Iberian wines – were shipped to Britain with remarkable consistency throughout the Napoleonic wars despite Portugal's enforced neutrality, subsequent invasion in 1808 by the French, and the long period of Anglo-Spanish hostility ended in the same year by Spain's discovery that Napoleon's intentions were less than friendly. What kept the trade alive during these years was continuing control of the seas, made irreversible by Nelson's victory at Trafalgar, the cape just 20 miles south of Cadiz where, on Napoleon's orders, a combined French and Spanish fleet sailed out from the sanctuary of the great sherry port to meet their nemesis on 21 October 1805. The battle made Britain safe from what had been a real threat of French invasion, and must have been cause for considerable relief among the shippers of Iberian wines, whose difficulties are well summed up by this circular of August 1805, sent out to customers by Sandeman:

> We beg leave to acquaint you, that a Convoy is now going out to Portugal, and to request the favour of your orders for our house at Porto, Thomas da Rocha Pinto and Sons, whose Prices for this opportunity, we subjoin; as also those of our house at Xerez, W. Lacosta and Lagarde ...

Sandeman's circular to customers of 19 August 1805, just before the Battle of Trafalgar.

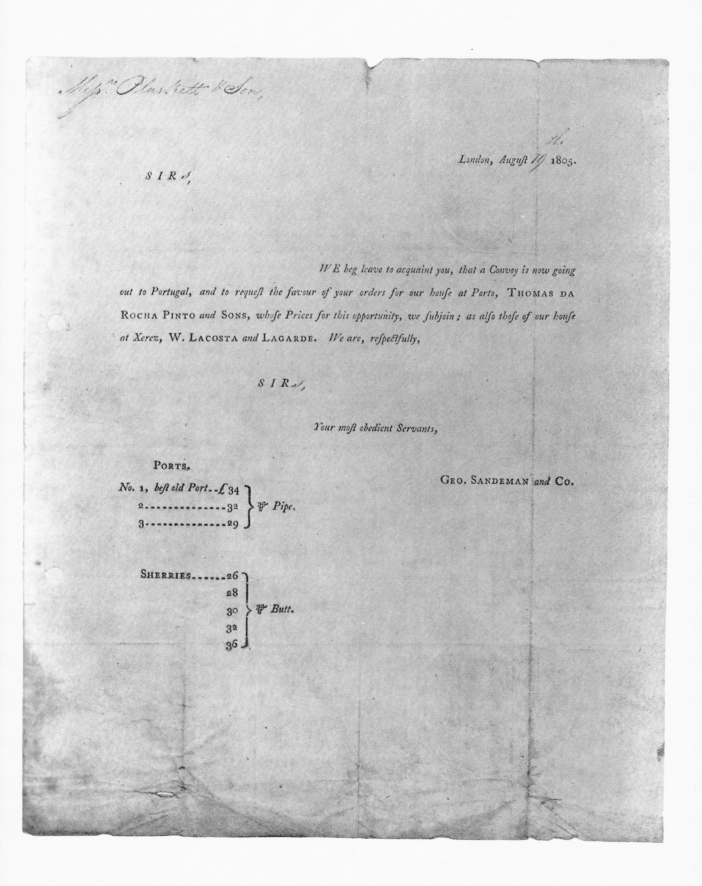

Messrs. Plaskett & Son,

London, August 19 1805.

S I R ,

WE beg leave to acquaint you, that a Convoy is now going out to Portugal, and to request the favour of your orders for our house at Porto, THOMAS DA ROCHA PINTO and SONS, whose Prices for this opportunity, we subjoin; as also those of our house at Xerez, W. LACOSTA and LAGARDE. We are, respectfully,

S I R ,

Your most obedient Servants,

GEO. SANDEMAN and CO.

PORTS.

No. 1, best old Port --£ 34 ⎫
2 --------------- 32   ⎬ ℣ Pipe.
3 --------------- 29   ⎭

SHERRIES ...... 26 ⎫
28   ⎬
30   ⎬ ℣ Butt.
32   ⎬
36   ⎭

LONDON, *April* 1809.

S I R

WE beg leave to acquaint you, that we continue to forward orders for PORT WINES, *to our friends* THOMAS DA ROCHA PINTO & SONS, *at Oporto, and for* SHERRIES, *to our partner, Mr.* GOODEN, *now at Cadiz; and that every exertion will be made under existing circumstances, to execute them to your satisfaction. We subjoin their shipping prices with those of our friends at Madeira and Teneriffe, and request the favour of your orders for them as well as for our friends at Lisbon, whose prices we shall also advise when fixed. We have a considerable supply of these, together with* CLARETS *and other Wines at this Port, which we beg to offer you at the prices annexed; and we remain, respectfully,*

S I R

Your most obedient Servants,

GEO. SANDEMAN, GOODEN & CO.

SHIPPING PRICES.

PORTS........*First quality* £34—*second* £32 ℣ *Pipe,* 9 *months, subject to any extra charge if the French are at Oporto.*

SHERRIES ....£28, 30, 32, 34, 36, 40 ℣ *Butt,* 3 *months.*
MADEIRA ....*London particular*......47 ℣ *Pipe,* 6 *months.*
VIDONIA *or* TENERIFFE............22 ℣ *Pipe,* 3 *months.*

PRICES of WINES in London, 3 *months.*

PORTS.......£95 *to* £ ℣ 138 *gal.*
SHERRY .....£90 *to* £98 ℣ 130 *gal.*
MADEIRA, *West-India and Brazil,* £110 *and* £112 ℣ 110 *gal.*
VIDONIA .....£ 78...℣ 120 *gal.*
LISBON.......£92.....℣ 140 *gal.—very old ditto* £94.
BUCELLAS £96
CARCAVELLA .£96 } ----℣ 140 *gal.*
MOUNTAIN ...£75......℣ 126 *gal.*
CLARET.......£88......℣ *Hhd.—or* £4 4 ℣ *doz.*

The Sandeman circular of April 1809 warned customers that there might be extra charges for port 'if the French are at Oporto'. The French were indeed at Oporto; Marshal Soult had taken the city on 29 March.

Victory at sea did not solve all the problems of the port and sherry trades. France invaded Portugal in 1807, with Spain's collusion, and aimed to close Lisbon and Oporto to British shipping in an extension of Napoleon's 'Continental System'. This scheme was intended to strangle Britain's trade with Europe – most of which was either occupied by, or in submission to, the armies of France. 'I mean to conquer the sea by land,' Bonaparte boasted, crowing at the prospect of British ships 'laden with useless wealth wandering the high seas, where they claim to be sole masters, vainly seeking a port to receive them.'

The Emperor's army was largely unopposed in its progress to Lisbon, but the success of the mission was brief. In the summer of 1808 a British expeditionary force landed at the Portuguese capital. Its commander was Sir Arthur Wellesley, who promptly routed the French, forcing them into a humiliating withdrawal from Portugal, and sparking off the five years of conflict we now know as the Peninsular War.

Napoleon refused to accept defeat and despatched a new army under the command of his most trusted officer, Marshal Soult, in 1809. Soult rapidly reoccupied the country, this time marching as far north as Oporto, which he seized on 29 March. Knowing the French were coming, the port trade shipped out as much of the wine as possible – at ruinous prices. Sandeman's circular to customers of that April showed admirable *sang froid* in the circumstances, quoting port shipping prices 'subject to any extra charge if the French are at Oporto'.

The French were not at Oporto long. Again, Wellesley had landed at Lisbon. Aided by the courageous men of the Portuguese resistance, he made a rapid march to the Douro River, crossed, and caught Soult completely unawares by appearing at Vila Nova de Gaia in May. In the fighting and retreat from the city, Soult lost 5,000 men, all his artillery – and his reputation for invincibility. In recognition of his remarkable victory, Wellesley was created Baron Douro – and Viscount Wellington.

The saving of the city was, not unnaturally, a cause for considerable joy among its people in general and the British in particular. 'Portonians went mad with delight,' wrote Rose Macaulay. 'They revelled and celebrated for days and nights on end; the British Factory entertained Wellington's officers, made them honorary members of the Factory (their names are entered in the Factory House book), and gave wine (quite too much) to the troops.'

George Sandeman was very probably among those hospitable revellers. He was travelling widely both in Spain and in Portugal at the time, by all accounts entirely undaunted by the war, making many friends among the British officers serving in Wellington's campaigns. He was well acquainted, too, with the Duke himself, and was a frequent guest at the headquarters mess behind the defensive lines at Torres Vedras – the impenetrable fortifications built immediately north of Lisbon where the last French army to invade Portugal was obliterated in 1810.

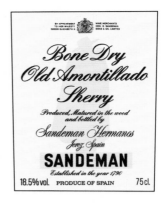

At one dinner in the mess, Sandeman confidently informed Wellington that the port they were drinking, the Sandeman 1797, was 'the finest ever known'. His opinion was clearly valued by another of the guests, General Calvert, Wellington's Quartermaster-general, who asked Sandeman to ship two pipes of the wine home for him. One of the pipes was presented by the general to the Duke of York, the Commander-in-chief of the Army. The Sandeman 1797 has since become known as the Duke of York's port, and is certainly one of the earliest of the classic vintages – as bottle-ageing of the wine was still then very much in its experimental stages.

That Sandeman should have had such high praise for the 1797 port puzzled the eminent wine writer H. Warner Allen. 'The odd thing about this judgement,' he wrote in a 1964 article, 'was that the 1797 vintage was officially described as "very bad, tawny" at a time when tawniness spelt damnation. I can find no other explanation for this contradiction than the belief that the vintage began well and ended in disaster and that the enterprising Mr Sandeman bought up all the fine wines already made before the weather broke.'

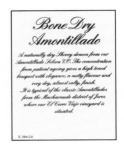

There are certainly no doubts that, as Walter Albert Sandeman put it, 'many a pipe of port from the Sandeman "Lodges" in Oporto played its part in making the lot of the British officer more endurable during the Peninsular War.' A letter from Colonel Bryan O'Toole to George Sandeman, written on 5 January 1815, delightfully illustrates the point:

> Your so kindly remembering the cold uncomfortable quarters I gave you in Elva is a thorough proof of the goodness of your heart. Colonel Prior forwarded to me your pipe of port, which is the best I ever drank. It arrived in pudding time, just before Christmas, when I had a dozen of friends to keep the holidays with me, and they found it so good that I could hardly get them out of my house yesterday. Your health, my good sir, was drank with three cheers in a bumper of it every day after our cheese.

In Spain, meanwhile, the war had not prevented Sandeman becoming thoroughly established in the sherry trade, with the arrival of George Sandeman's partner, James Gooden, at Cadiz in 1809. But early in 1810, the French invaded the region, seizing Jerez and laying siege to Cadiz. Not until the late summer of 1812, when Wellington took Madrid and French forces were recalled, could the production of sherry resume. Sadly, the French troops had not shown the restraint on this occasion that George Sandeman had so commended when writing to his father back in 1796. Many of the vineyards surrounding Jerez had been battlefields, stocks of wine had been plundered in two-and-a-half years of occupation. The peace that followed brought a slow recovery for the trade – with boom times not far ahead.

Chapter VI

Sandeman in London – the Early Years

George Sandeman Jnr (1816–1860), eldest son of the founder.

To further the good relations with the military that he made during the Peninsular War, George Sandeman could not have chosen a better location for the offices that were to be the firm's headquarters from 1805 until 1969. Number 20 St Swithin's Lane and number 13 Sherborne Lane, the house backing on to it and which became the private residence, lay on the route from the London docks into town. The house was always open to officers returning from the war with despatches for the Foreign Office. The many friends Sandeman entertained there no doubt provided him with much of the commercial intelligence that enabled the firm to prosper in spite of the obvious exigencies of the time.

Back in 1790, George Sandeman had written home to Perth predicting that his new enterprise would make him 'a moderate fortune to retire with, which I expect will be in the course of nine years . . . but some lucky stroke may possibly reduce it to five or six.' This achievement seems, in the end, to have taken him seven years, for on 12 October 1797 Perth honoured him with the freedom of the city – an emphatic confirmation that young George, still aged only 33, had indeed become a man of substance. He returned the compliment to his native city a few years later by playing a leading role in financing the Perth Academy, which opened in 1807. (Another scion of the family, Professor Archibald Sandeman of Owen College, Manchester, provided the bequest that founded Perth's Sandeman Public Library in 1898.)

The London business seems to have resided only temporarily at 24 Old Jewry after George Sandeman took a lease there in 1794, for one of the firm's circulars, dated 10 January 1798, bears the address Tom's Coffee House – and the same address is listed for George Sandeman in the London Post Office Directory for 1800. By this time, George and his brother David had amicably ended their partnership (David had represented the firm in Scotland, but now turned to his first interest, banking).

In 1800 George took on the first of what was to be a series of partners from outside the Sandeman family, Samuel Sketchley Robinson, who brought with him important extra capital for the expansion of the business. The firm now took on the name Sandeman Robinson & Co., but only until 1805 when Robinson died and the style became Geo. Sandeman & Co.

In 1809 came a new partner, James Gooden – and thus the name Geo. Sandeman Gooden & Co. – but within the year he had departed for Cadiz as the firm's resident partner there, shipping sherries home under the Sandeman name. In 1812, again in need of more working capital for the growing business,

Overleaf: 13 Sherborne Lane, backing on to Sandeman's St Swithin's Lane headquarters, became George Sandeman's home in 1805.

The original Freedom of the City granted by Perth to George Sandeman, 'Merchant in London' on 12 October 1797.

W. Niven f. Del. 1873 Sc. 1900

George Sandeman took his cousin, John Carey Forster, into partnership. As well as importing wines, the firm in these early years also did a considerable trade with the West Indies, Central America and Mexico, exporting British linens, cotton goods and other manufactured products in exchange for valued New World bounty such as silver bullion. The Company's growing wealth – apparently unaffected by the failure of its bankers, Moffat & Kensington & Co. in 1812, after which Sandeman took his business to the Bank of England – now brought it, for a time, into banking and insurance.

Until 1828, when James Gooden died, the firm was named Geo. Sandeman Gooden & Forster, becoming Sandeman Forster & Co. until the retirement of John Forster Jnr in 1856.

As well as the private residence at Sherborne Lane, the founder took a 'country' home, too, at Highbury. Now very much part of metropolitan London, the borough was then largely open countryside and, as George Sandeman frequently complained, 'a perilous journey' away from the City. The property was the Sandeman family home, a farm but not apparently run on any commercial basis. It appears to have been inherited from the founder by George Glas Sandeman, his nephew and successor as head of the firm. A letter to George Glas in 1844, from his friend Mr Hennessy of the great Cognac company, cheerfully expresses the hope that 'Mrs Sandeman and all your children are well and that the farming establishment at Highbury is a source of health if not profits'.

But it was at St Swithin's Lane that the founder held court. Just around the corner from the original cellar George Sandeman rented in 1790, the building and the Sherborne Lane house backing it had been built by the Drapers' Company over an ancient vault, providing dry and cool cellars ideal for ageing

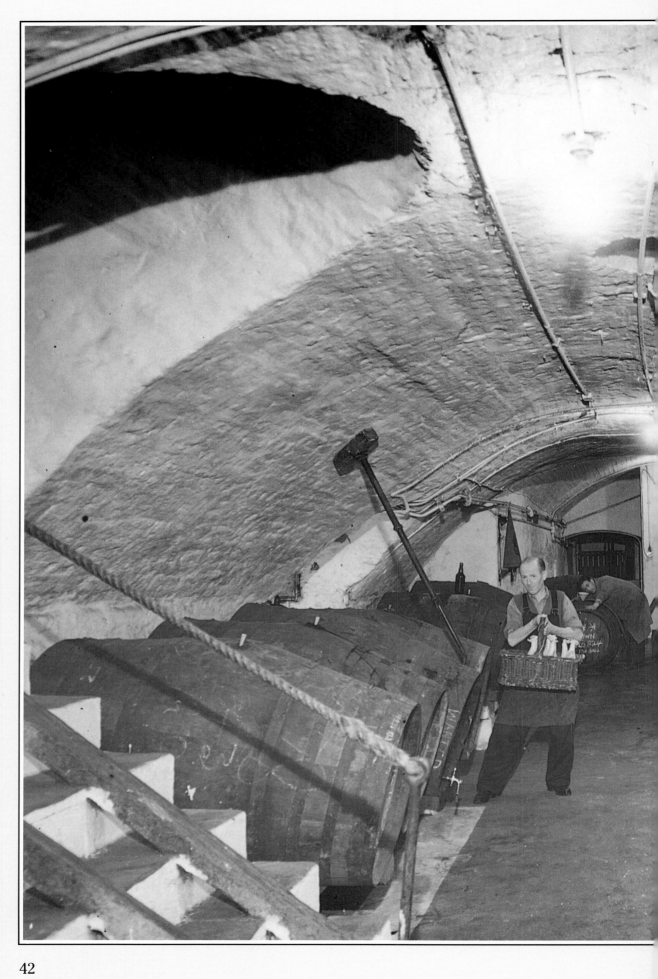

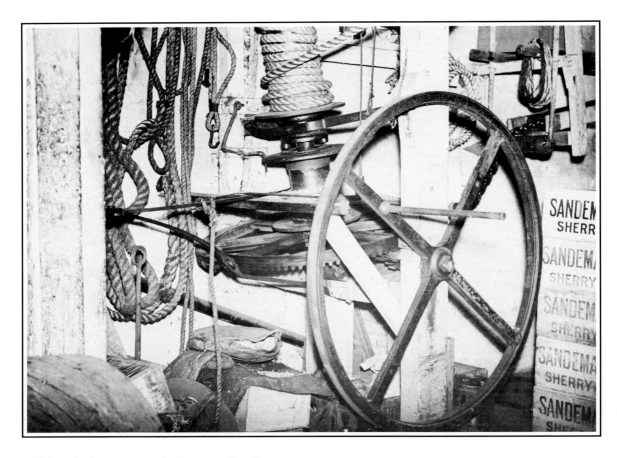

old bottled ports and sherries in the constant temperature. Testimony to ancient origins of the site was found in the 1870s when building workers discovered an oblong chamber cut into the clay below the floor of the vaults. Its walls lined with chalk blocks bound together by Roman mortar mixed with flints, the chamber had two underground passages leading off it, both long ago blocked up, but one obviously leading in the direction of the River Thames. The passageways and chamber were probably part of a defence system in Roman times, and date from the first century AD.

Number 20 St Swithin's Lane happens to be on the boundary of two parishes, St Swithin and St Mary Abchurch, as George Sandeman would no doubt have discovered from the lead boundary mark, dated 1784, displayed in the vaults. The cellars, as he was also soon to discover, were among the boundary points in the City where a charming ritual was regularly performed: Beating the Bounds. The custom was said to derive from the Roman festival of the god Terminus, Guardian of Fields and Landmarks, in which the children who tended flocks were marched around the boundaries of their communities' grazing land and given thrashings along the way to concentrate their minds on their precise limits. By the last century this had evolved into a gentler pantomime of beating the boundary marks with willow sticks. The tradition is still keenly observed in the City today, as it was throughout Sandeman's time there in a fashion delightfully described in a company memoire of 1949:

The Capital Patent Crane at 20 St Swithin's Lane was installed by George Sandeman in 1805 when he took over the lease, and remained fully functional right until the time the company moved to other premises in 1969, having hoisted countless thousands of casks of wine in and out of the cellars. Listed as an item of special historic interest, the crane was presented by Sandeman to the Drapers' Company, owners of the St Swithin's Lane freehold.

Pages 42 and 43: The Sandeman cellars at 20 St Swithin's Lane in the 1950s. The site had been first excavated by the Romans.

On the day selected by either Parish the Clergy, Beadle and other officials in their colourful robes accompanied by many young people and representatives of the Press proclaim their ancient rights and invade Sandemans' Vaults with no little hilarity and merriment. Here as may be expected, the procession is somewhat tardy in its forward movement. All are welcomed with old-fashioned hospitality and as in the days of the Terminalia the grown-ups are entertained with medieval bumpers of fine Sherry and Port in accordance with tradition and in a manner appropriate to the surroundings.

The tradition of hospitality at St Swithin's Lane ran deep and could be, as this letter from a nephew of George Sandeman's indicated in 1814, a testing experience:

I dined at my uncle's in St Swithin's Lane, where I reside, about six o'clock. Such late hours I dislike, otherwise things were quite agreeable. The party consisted of six gentlemen, who seemed more or less connected with the French trade. We had a variety of fine wines, claret, and other kinds, whose names were quite new to me. I was tempted to take five or six glasses of Madeira, besides some others. Not being accustomed to such liquors, I felt some degree of fever through the night; my head was not affected at all.

The prosperity of the firm at this time seems remarkable in the light of the effect the Napoleonic Wars – and the war in the Peninsula in particular – had on the trade. Prices for all commodities in Britain doubled between 1790 and 1815. It was by far the worst inflation the country was to experience until after the Second World War, and reflected the enormous cost of 20 years' conflict with France. Prices quoted by Sandeman in London show the trend, for example, for best-quality port, per pipe, on board ship at Oporto (and thus exclusive of shipping and insurance charges). In 1793, the price was £23, in 1805 it had reached £34 and ten years later £50. Sales, unsurprisingly, slumped. The sherry trade suffered a similar fate, with Sandeman prices per butt at Cadiz moving from £17 for young wine in 1796 to £37 in 1818.

In spite of these unprecedented price rises, demand appears to have stayed well ahead of supply. Harvests in both the Douro Valley and in the Jerez vineyards were depleted by the war, and stocks of old wines had been sold off to prevent them falling into French hands. As a letter of 12 March 1816 from the Oporto office to London put it: 'We think there will be no occasion to make sacrifices to get rid of our stock as it will not exceed 800 pipes altogether.'

By 1820, prices were easing back. A circular of 1824 offered best port at £38 and young sherry at £28. As the farmers restored the vineyards and new businesses were established in place of those that had failed during the war, vigorous competition brought improved quality in the wines. The sherry trade in particular was on the threshold of its finest hour, the middle decades of the nineteenth century. With faultless

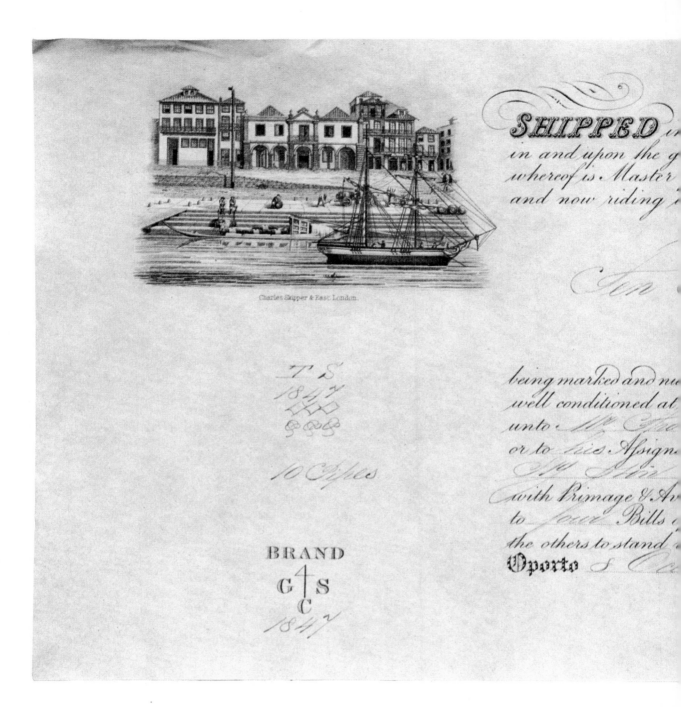

The stylish illustration of the Sandeman lodges on the company's bills of lading (this one is dated 1851) was drawn by Edwin Sandeman, a son of the founder of the firm.

timing, Sandeman made an exclusive agency agreement with one of the top sherry houses, Julian Pemartin, in 1822.

By now, George Sandeman was among the best-known figures in the City, not just for his famous business but for an undoubted eccentricity. He is said to have been the last merchant to appear in the Royal Exchange ('On 'Change' in the City jargon of the day) dressed in the eighteenth-century style complete with breeches, top boots and white wig. The latter adornment earned him the affectionate nickname of Old Cauliflower.

In 1835, by now 70 years old, the founder was living in Brussels, presumably retired from actively managing the firm, but still the senior partner. He remained at Number 2 Place Royale, then owned by Viscomte Cobert and now Number 7 and part of Belgium's foreign ministry, until he died on 2

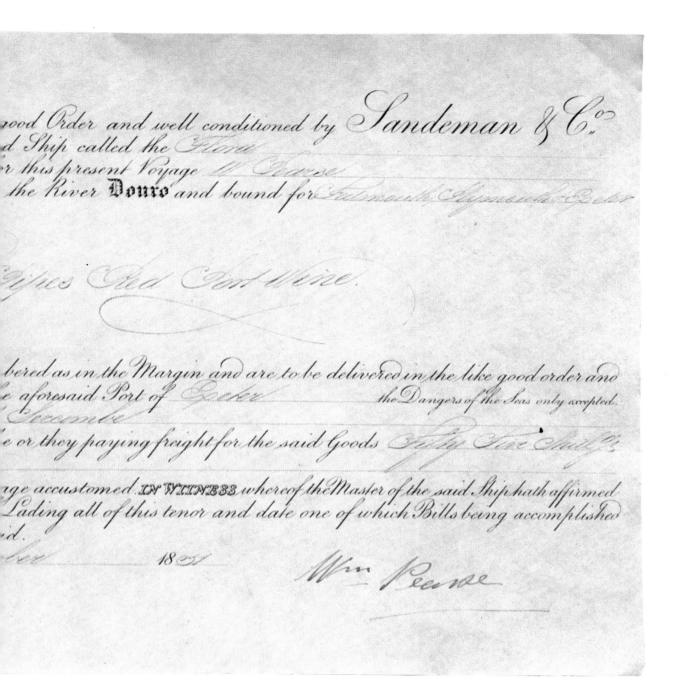

February 1841. He was buried in the Quartier Leopold Cemetery. In 1888, the grave had to be moved and George Sandeman's remains were reburied in the cemetery at Evere, just north-east of Brussels. Along with him was buried his daughter Ellen who had been moved too. She had died in Brussels back in 1834, aged only 14.

George Sandeman's eldest son, also George, worked in the business, but did not succeed his father as head of the firm. The founder apparently preferred his nephew, George Glas Sandeman, for the job. Already a partner by the time of his uncle's death, it is from George Glas that all subsequent heads of the company have been directly descended.

The founder's first marriage (he married again in later life) produced eight children who achieved maturity. The above-mentioned George died childless in 1860. Next was Alfred,

The boot and flogger – the eighteenth-century precursor to today's automated corking technology. The bottle was held in the boot and the cork driven in with the hardwood flogger. This means was used for corking Sandeman's last London-bottled vintage port, the 1955.

Henry Sandeman, 1829–1852, youngest son of the founder.

described in one Sandeman history as 'at one time a most successful squatter in Australia' – in other words an early settler who acquired his vast sheep station near Sydney simply by staking a claim on it. It was Alfred's son Edgar, born 1860, who had the great good sense to preserve the founder's earliest letters, which tell so much of how the House of Sandeman was created. The third son, Edwin, worked for the firm in Oporto. He was a particularly talented draughtsman, whose work includes the fine engraving of the Sandeman Lodges that for many years appeared on the company's bills of lading (see page 46). Youngest son was Henry who, like many of the family, chose a military career. He was commissioned into the Royal Engineers in 1847.

Of George Sandeman's daughters, Mary Ann, the eldest, married John Thomson, manager of the firm in Oporto. It was a posting she did not apparently relish. Her brother George wrote in an 1855 letter to Alfred in Australia that 'Mary Ann and Sophia [her sister] dreaded returning to Oporto' adding 'I am not surprised at it'. Alfred wrote back: 'Neither am I. I would rather live in the bush than there.' Just what it was that the founder's heirs so disliked about Oporto is not detailed in any of the letters still in existence. There were two other daughters, Fanny and Laura. The latter stayed at home to take care of their mother, who died in 1851.

The Sandeman Trade Mark
The trade mark embossed on bottles of Sandeman wines bears the initials GSC, for George Sandeman & Co. The firm traded under this name from 1805 to 1809, so it is likely that the brand dates from that time. It has been in use on company documents at least since the 1840s, to identify Sandeman ports, and has since been adapted for other wines such as the sherries shipped under the mark, for Sandeman Buck & Co., between 1879 and 1923.

The brand – in the true meaning of the word, as it would originally have been branded into the wine casks – was registered as a trade mark on 23 March 1877. Recording marks had only been possible since the previous year, when the first Trade Marks Registration Act was placed on the statute books. The Sandeman brand is consequently one of the oldest registered trade marks still in use. The name Sandeman and the Don trade mark are now registered in 130 countries around the world.

Chapter VII

Sandeman in Oporto – the Nineteenth Century

The Sandeman lodges have looked out across the Vila Nova de Gaia waterfront to the precipitous and picturesquely overcrowded slopes of Oporto for nearly two centuries. The handsome arcaded building is believed to be the work of architect Joaquim da Costa Lima Sampaio, who also designed the city's Royal Palace and was partly responsible for the Factory House. The lodges, with a well-proportioned facade of one upper storey modestly pedimented over a five-arch loggia, may have been built as early as 1797, but it was probably not until 1813–14 that Sandeman took possession. Official records show that the firm's first year as an exporter (and thus the first time it would have needed lodges in Gaia) was 1813, when it bought 26 pipes from Noble Perkins. The business grew very quickly, with exports rising to 541 pipes in 1814, according to the books of the old Wine Company, through which all purchases then had to be made.

Sandeman was already a well-established name in the port trade. Two decades earlier, the firm had been representing the shippers Charles Offley & Co. in London and Scotland, and had since imported wines from Thomas da Rocha Pinto & Sons before becoming a shipper in its own right. The wines the company bought from the farmers 60 or more miles upriver in the heartland of the vine-growing country could now be delivered direct to the Sandeman quay. It would come in the hefty 550-litre casks known to the Portuguese as *pipas* – and thus, to the British, as pipes – piled precariously high aboard the little ships of the Douro, the *barcos rabelos*.

In those early years, the stocks of wine held in the lodges (so-called after the Portuguese *lojas*, or storehouses) would vary from a few hundred to several thousand, according to the wild fluctuations in the quantity – and quality – of port available from one vintage to the next. Building up a stock was, of course, the only sure way the shipper had of getting into that ideal position of assuring customers a dependable supply year after year.

As a letter of May 1814 from Sandeman in Oporto to St Swithin's Lane reveals, port at the time was very much a seller's market:

> Our letters from the Douro mention that almost all wines (of the 1813 vintage) have been bought up. Here also a great many wines have been bought up already and the general idea is that wines will gradually advance (in price) all year. We have bought 100 pipes from Mr Forrester and as many more from Mr Pinto which will make about 800 pipes in all our lodges ... we are of opinion that we could sell all the wines we have got to considerable profit as the market is at present.

Overleaf: The Sandeman *barco rabelo* at Vila Nova de Gaia.

Each spring, the Oporto shippers would travel up to the Douro Valley to attend the annual wine fair at Regua, visit the growers, taste the wines made from the previous autumn's harvest, and make what purchases they could – according to the amount of wine the official Wine Company permitted for

SANTA MARINHA

sale. (The Wine Company first bought all the wine it considered would be required for the home market. The better-quality port was usually allocated for sale to the exporters, at higher prices.)

In February and March 1816, George G. Sandeman made the Douro tour in search of the fruits of the great harvest of the previous year – known long since, of course, as the Waterloo Vintage. He found that the Wine Company, 'contrary to their usual custom', had this time 'bought a very large proportion of the finest lodges in the country. Of all the lodges we bought last year scarcely 100 pipes remained out of the Company.' George G. Sandeman was able to report, fortunately, that 'we have bought 270 pipes, which will make a very good lot'. As for older wines being offered by stockholding farmers and speculators, he took a dim view of what he had seen: 'The quantity of wines now for sale up the Country does not much exceed 10,000 pipes, of which the greatest proportion are bad.'

Delivery of the new purchases began straight away. The pipes were sent down from the wineries on ox carts, the basic design of which had remained unchanged since Roman times. So steep are most of the routes down the plunging ravines of the Upper Douro to the waterside that the carts could take only one cask per trip. The oxen had to inch down the unmade tracks, propelled on by the great weight behind them – a full pipe weighs half a ton – for hour after hour. The piercing din made by the grinding of the cart's iron wheels against their axles had the compensating benefit, according to local lore, of frightening away not just the wolves, but the devil himself.

The next stage of the wine's journey might have been a more rapid progress – but it had its hazards. The *barco rabelo* boats

were flat-bottomed, with an upswept tapering high prow and raised after-deck from which the steersman could operate the mighty tiller. Some *rabelos* had oarsmen, others simply a square sail at the single mast. The capacity of these elegant craft then ranged from just a few pipes to 70, 80 or more. It took remarkable skills to navigate the *rabelo* through the numerous treacherous shallows and rapids of the river – and it comes as no surprise that the brave men aboard were, as one nineteenth-century observer put it, 'very strict in the observance of their religious duties, and whenever the image of a saint is passed, perched on the summit of the cliffs bordering the river, they bare their heads and repeat a short prayer'.

The new wine, once safely delivered to the lodges, might be either blended with that of previous vintages to make basic wine of a consistent style, or with other purchases from the same year to make true vintage port. A year or so later, the new wine would be ready for first shipment. In April 1817, Sandeman Oporto were informing Sandeman London of their high opinion of the 1815 wines now starting to reach customers: 'We think those shipt for Flemyng Wines remarkably good 1815's and have charged them £42 which we hope they will not object to.'

It was a prosperous time, but not entirely a tranquil one in a country which experienced countless political upheavals in the aftermath of the Napoleonic Wars. The revolution of 1820, which removed a British officer, Marshal Beresford (a customer of Sandeman), from command of the Portuguese army and ended British political influence within the nation, was a bloodless one in Oporto. But the war of 1832 between rivals for the throne, the royal brothers Dom Miguel and Dom Pedro, turned out very much more dangerous for the city – which

proclaimed itself for the liberal Pedro and came under siege from the Miguelites.

It lasted more than a year, cutting Oporto off from the vineyards, bringing factional fighting into the streets and disrupting the port trade in no uncertain fashion. A Royal Navy squadron in the harbour did, however, mean communications were kept open with the outside world, enabling Sandeman to send sanguine messages such as this letter of September 1832 to their London bankers, N. M. Rothschild, on the urgent matter of some outstanding bills: 'We should find no difficulty in discounting these Bills, if we could procure satisfactory Paper on London to remit you, but this City being in a state of siege every description of business is at a stand...However, you

may rest assured we will not lose the first opportunity of remitting you.'

In the following May, this letter to the London office spoke in matter-of-fact terms of the continuing siege:

In Vila Nova things continue for the moment quieter. The Serra artillery [the hilltop Serra convent, overlooking Gaia, was an important Miguelite stronghold] since our late advices, has only injured the roof and some of the inside arches, and for the last few days only musket shots and at a rather greater distance. We have still the Piquet [guard] stationed with us, and no security against more mischief.

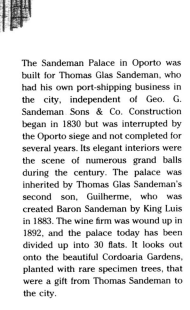

The Sandeman Palace in Oporto was built for Thomas Glas Sandeman, who had his own port-shipping business in the city, independent of Geo. G. Sandeman Sons & Co. Construction began in 1830 but was interrupted by the Oporto siege and not completed for several years. Its elegant interiors were the scene of numerous grand balls during the century. The palace was inherited by Thomas Glas Sandeman's second son, Guilherme, who was created Baron Sandeman by King Luis in 1883. The wine firm was wound up in 1892, and the palace today has been divided up into 30 flats. It looks out onto the beautiful Cordoaria Gardens, planted with rare specimen trees, that were a gift from Thomas Sandeman to the city.

Sandeman seems to have weathered the inevitable damage and looting very well. It was now emphatically the largest port shipper. In 1835, its shipments amounted to 4,580 pipes – about 12 per cent of the total port exports for the year of 38,468 pipes. No other shipper even approached this figure.

While Sandeman survived intact, the old Wine Company did not fare so well. As it became known that the Miguelites would soon have to lift their siege and march south to Lisbon (which had just fallen to Pedro), it was clear that the company – controlled by Miguelites, and corrupt Miguelites at that – would shortly be up for grabs. In August 1833, days before the siege ended, a group of 'neutral' French officers – in fact supporters of Miguel – laid explosives in the company lodges and blew the whole lot up. Their motive was apparently to prevent the stocks falling into Pedroist (in other words, British) hands. In the enormous explosion that resulted, 27,000 pipes of wine were destroyed. The subsequent fire might very well have spread through all of Vila Nova de Gaia had it not been for the quick action of one of the Sandemans – probably George Glas – who crossed over the Douro to raise the alarm in Oporto. He returned with Captain Glascock, the naval squadron commander, who with his officers and men – assisted by the shippers' workers – just got the flames under control in time. 'Wine and brandy in boiling and flaming torrents were running in rapid streams down the different lanes leading to the lodges', Glascock recalled. 'It was impossible to approach the scalding vapour in the air.'

It was the last straw for the Wine Company. The new Portuguese constitution of 1834 suspended it. Although only four years later it was reinstated – in the wake of the free-for-all that caused the quality (and price) of some wines to plummet – it never again had its former monopolistic powers and was finally laid to rest in 1865. The regulation of the port trade is now the responsibility of the Port Wine Institute.

The closing of the Wine Company meant that port's reputation now rested firmly with the shippers, among whom a great controversy was soon to break out over the very methods which gave the wine its unique character. Joseph James Forrester, nephew of Offley Forrester partner James Forrester (one of George Sandeman's closest friends in Oporto), complained very publicly that port had 'fallen in the estimation of persons really capable of judging of wine'. Port, young Forrester proposed, should not be fortified in mid-fermentation at all. Rather than a 'black, strong and sweet' wine it should be a natural table wine. He inveighed, too, against the continuing practices of sweetening the wine with sugar, and deepening its colour with elderberries.

J. J. Forrester's views did not prevail, but his pleas for improved standards in the vineyards and lodges certainly had a salutary influence on the newly liberated trade – who soon forgave him for the haranguings to which he had submitted them. For his subsequent services to the port wine industry, including pioneering work in viticulture and his inspired cartography of the Douro, Forrester was granted the title of Baron in 1855.

Lieutenant-Colonel John Glas Sandeman, as a subaltern in the 1st Royal Dragoons, took part in the Charge of the Heavy Brigade at Balaclava. Younger brother of Albert George Sandeman, he served as the firm's resident partner in Oporto for a time, and was one of the original partners in Geo. G. Sandeman Sons & Co., along with Albert George and two younger brothers, George Glas and Fleetwood.

LIEUT. COL. JOHN. GLAS. SANDEMAN. M.V.O
SUB OFFICER.   ROYAL BODY GUARD.
GENTLEMAN AT ARMS.
From Sketch for Royal Diamond Jubilee Picture.

Among Forrester's achievements was his work on the fungal vine disease oidium, for which he pioneered the classic treatment (with sulphur) almost as soon as it first appeared in the Douro in the 1850s. But not before the disease, as this Sandeman letter to a New York customer of November 1855 reveals, had caused devastation in the vineyards: 'We are sorry to inform you that the result of this year's vintage has proved even worse than was expected, the quality being the worst and the quantity made the smallest ever remembered – as imputed at about 8,000 pipes instead 80,000 pipes in average years.'

As soon as the oidium was overcome, another pestilence followed – namely the phylloxera, the parasitic insect that infests and kills vines. First found in the Douro in 1868, it was

Members of the Factory House in the Rua Nova dos Inglezes, painted by Baron Forrester in 1834.

the mid-1880s before the only effective answer to phylloxera was found. This was to replant the vineyards with American rootstocks, which were resistant to the pest. By this time, the Douro vineyards had been devastated – along with those of virtually all of Europe.

After so many years of prosperity, the Douro farmers were hit very hard. John Forrester, writing to Albert Sandeman after a vineyard tour in October 1876, reported that 'the farmers poor fellows have got very much less than last year, and with reduced prices I do not see how they can continue to cultivate the vine. Many of them talk of planting tobacco, and I have no doubt they would if they could obtain the consent of the Government.'

Overleaf: The Sandeman schooner *Hoopoe* was built in 1865 and operated by the company for ten years. As well as carrying wines from Cadiz and Oporto, the elegant 75-foot vessel did frequent service as a collier ship – carrying coals from Newcastle at 10 shillings a ton. Sandeman sold the *Hoopoe* to the Oporto firm Charles Coverlay & Co. in 1875. In October 1878, *en route* to Oporto out of Devon, she was lost in the English Channel, with all hands.

Sandeman and the Factory House

Sandeman has been a member of the British Association – more familiarly known by the name of its grand premises in Oporto's Rua dos Inglezes (the 'Street of the English'), the Factory House – from its earliest days. The year 1990 is the bicentenary of the Factory House as well as that of the House of Sandeman.

The firm, one of the 12 members of this most exclusive of 'clubs' today, has supplied it with wine as far back as the records go. The oldest surviving cellar book, of 1831, lists 11 shippers' wines in the Factory House bins, Sandeman included. It is a reflection of the perils of the port trade that of the other ten names, only two remain in business today.

Sandeman's membership was interrupted in 1863 when the firm resigned in protest at the system by which subscriptions were collected, namely a levy per pipe of port shipped. As Sandeman was by far the largest shipper, it paid a very much higher subscription than any other member firm – and took exception to doing so. Four other major firms – Cockburn, Croft, Offley and Smith Woodhouse – felt similarly aggrieved and resigned too. As there were then only 11 members (there are just 12 even today), it is something of a tribute to the resolve – not to say obstinacy – of the Factory House that it held out until 1875 before changing the rules in order to lure the five firms back again.

Cabel Roope, Treasurer of the British Association, wrote to Sandeman on 22 December 1875, proposing that the firm rejoin. The reply, dated Christmas Eve, took an ingenuous tone, thanking the members for their kind proposal, but enquiring just how things stood: 'Being unacquainted with the rules of the British Association would you kindly inform us what may be the amount of Entrance Fee for each member – and as no member of our Firm has had the honour of being a member of the Association, perhaps you could favour us with a copy of the rules and by-laws.'

Strange as it may seem that no member of Sandeman had been a Factory House member at that time, this statement was nevertheless true, as George Glas Sandeman – presumably the firm's only member – had died during the period of disaffection, in 1868.

On 7 February 1876, Sandeman agreed to resume as a member 'under an arrangement by which all firms, being members, are to pay the same subscription and to enjoy equal rights and privileges'.

It is sad, of course, that George Glas Sandeman has not lived to enjoy the reconciliation. No doubt he would be pleased to know that today, among the portraits of distinguished members on view in the Factory House's elegant drawing room is one of himself – presented by his successors in the firm in 1953.

The House of Sandeman is one of today's 12 member firms, represented by the sixth generation of the family, the present Chairman David Patrick Sandeman and his brother Timothy Walter Sandeman who preceded him as head of the Company from 1959 to 1982.

At this time, Sandeman still owned no vineyards in the Douro, and so faced considerably fewer problems than the numerous shippers who had bought extensively in the valley. The firm, indeed, seemed particularly well set up at the time, as the writer Henry Vizetelly, who visited Sandeman in 1877, was able to report at considerable length in his book *Facts about Port*:

The Sandeman lodges around 1870, with the hilltop Serra convent in the background.

> Embarking at the ferry stairs at the foot of the Rua do São João, a couple of minutes suffice to row us across the Douro . . . immediately in front of us is a granite building with an open arcade below . . . On the principal doorway a small tablet, having a miniature representation of the Union Jack, in one corner, notifies that the edifice is British property, the owners being Messrs G. G. Sandeman Sons & Co., the eminent Port wine shippers, whose names for half-a-century past have regularly headed the Oporto shipping list. Here the firm have their offices, presenting somewhat of the antiquated appearance of a substantial merchant's counting-house of the last century, and

Right: The visitor reception centre at the lodges in Vila Nova de Gaia. Annually, thousands of visitors are shown over the lodges and wine museum, where they can linger over a glass of port.

Overleaf: Inside the lodges, around 1870.

adjoining is a network of lodges, in which their extensive stock of wine is stored. These comprise a series of irregular constructions, including numerous galleries or 'cumes', as they are technically termed, communicating occasionally with others by means of lofty arches, and many of them having all the appearance of great age. Fungi overspread the damper walls, rude, ponderous, blackened beams support their pointed roofs, and light usually is but sparingly admitted through small barred windows and diminutive skylights. Venerable-looking pipes full of the bright ruby-tinted potent wine of the Upper Douro are ranged in seemingly endless rows and in double and triple tiers, with here and there a tramway to facilitate the transport of the casks from one lodge to another. No special system of arrangement appears to be observed, wines of various ages, quality, and value frequently being stored for convenience under the same roof. Brawny barefooted matulas are threading their way between the long files of casks, balancing canecos, or wooden pitchers, full of wine deftly on their heads, or emptying them into rows of pipes which are being got ready for shipment. Most of the lodges contain huge vats, in which new wines on their arrival from the Upper Douro, after being carefully classed, are equally carefully blended, only vintage wines from particularly prized quintas being kept intact.

Vizetelly now passes on to the further Sandeman lodges at the rear, describing them as:

gloomy-looking stores, comprising a range of long low cumes, each divided into a couple of aisles by a series of arches. As port wine is believed to mature less perfectly when subject to the influence of light, these stores have but few windows or skylights. Walls and timbers alike are blackened by the constantly-evaporating alcohol, and monster cobwebs hang in fantastic festoons before the dingy windows and from the dark, decaying rafters. The

Sandeman

66

Precious stocks of old tawny port.

Left: The wine museum at the
Sandeman lodges.

stock of wine in these united stores is larger than that held by any other shipper, and in the spring of the year will probably amount to little short of 10,000 pipes.

The company had indeed grown very rapidly during the nineteenth century. In 1870, according to the official figures, Sandeman shipped 3,781 pipes (2 million litres), accounting for about 9 per cent of all port exports for the year. Of about 100 other shippers, only Cockburn remotely rivalled this level of business, with shipments for the year of 3,022 pipes.

While the fortunes of port, and of Sandeman, had fluctuated throughout the century, it is extraordinary against the background of late-twentieth-century inflation to see how steady the prices remained during the 1800s. Sandeman's Superior Old Port, for example, while it did rise in price during the Napoleonic Wars from around £30 to around £50 per pipe on board at Oporto, was back to £38 in 1824. In 1853, it was being offered at £36 to £38. By the 1890s the price had climbed to between £44 and £52 – no higher than its 1815 price, in spite of the continuing effects in the Douro vineyards of phylloxera and, almost as bad, the mildew that struck in 1893.

For the port trade as a whole, business gradually improved through the latter half of the century. Average annual exports moved from 33,000 pipes in the 1860s to 52,000 in the 1870s and 60,000 in the 1880s. It must be said that in the latter years much of the wine involved did not come from the officially

Vintage ports maturing in bins.

demarcated Alto Douro vineyards (as the Port Wine Institute has wryly pointed out, the peak export figure of the century, 75,000 pipes, was achieved in the year when 'the ravages of the phylloxera were at their most severe', 1886). The fact that port supplies were largely uninterrupted during the period of wine shortages throughout Europe was certainly an element in bringing the Oporto trade into the twentieth century in such a prosperous condition.

Chapter VIII

Port – the Making of the Wine

The processes of port production were gradually updated throughout the nineteenth century, and have continued that development ever since. But the principles of making the wine have remained the same.

The ports George Sandeman was offering to his customers in the 1790s were very much in the style of the wines we know today. The region from which the grapes could be harvested had already been demarcated, and the method of fortifying the wine with brandy in mid-fermentation was well established. And with the introduction in the late 1700s of the cylindrical, stackable bottle, the era of bottle-aged vintages had begun.

The defined grape-growing region of the Douro Valley, first marked out by Pombal in the 1750s, extends from about 60 miles upriver from Oporto to within a few miles of the Spanish border. The zone was increased to its present size in 1801 and now covers 1,500 square miles. Of this, only a fraction is actually under vine – about 10 per cent.

Looking up the steep hillsides that rise directly from the river, it is hard to imagine how the first farmers here can have assumed that this forbidding landscape might be a suitable place for vine-growing at all. The plunging slopes have to be cut deeply to form level terraces, on each of which a mere two or three rows of vines can be planted. The ground is formed of the slate-like stone called schist, which must be broken and churned up to become the 'soil' of the vineyard – in fact a very good growing medium for vines as the stony ground allows winter rains to run through to the impermeable rock beneath. This gives the roots a reservoir of moisture to see them through the torrid summers in which rainfall can be minimal and temperatures may reach 44°C (110°F).

The terraces, traditionally walled with cut schist, are the only means of preventing the erosion of the cultivated ground. The torrential rains would simply wash the loose stone down the slopes and into the river. The new vineyards being created in the Douro today, such as Sandeman's extension to the newly acquired Quinta do Vau, still depend on terracing to make the cultivation of the best land possible. Though the bulldozer may have replaced the pick and shovel, the principle remains unchanged.

It is an adage of viticulture that the poorer the soil is, the higher the quality of the fruit harvested from it is likely to be. In the Douro, probably the toughest wine-growing region in the world, this paradoxical belief is unquestionably true. Ground that is almost pure schist does produce the best grapes – but in very small quantities.

Different vine varieties, of course, yield larger or smaller

Touriga Nacional is the finest of all Douro varieties. Deep-coloured, with intense aroma and good sugar content, it has similarities with the great Cabernet Sauvignon of Bordeaux. A low yielder.

Pick of the bunch: illustrated on this and the next two pages are the five grape varieties that today dominate in the Alto Douro vineyards – between them accounting for all the new plantings, for example, at Sandeman's Quinta do Vau vineyard, as per the recommendation of the Ministry of Agriculture in Oporto.

Carefully constructed terracing makes maximum use of the best terrain, and prevents the topsoil eroding through landslip.

harvests of grapes, so the farmer chooses appropriately, according to his needs for quality and quantity. There are 51 varieties approved for the region. Of these, only 15 are recommended and now only 5 are being planted in new vineyards. It goes without saying that those which produce the finest fruit tend to yield the smallest crops. The Touriga Nacional, widely held to be the premier variety, and a very important constituent in the best wine's aroma and flavour, produces only a third of the fruit that some heavy-cropping vines will bear. Farmers are not free, however, simply to plant the most abundantly productive varieties. The Port Wine Institute limits each vineyard, according to its individual characteristics, to the amount of wine it can produce as port in any one year. That allocation is made partly according to the varieties of vines planted; better-quality, lower-yielding vines bring the grower the benefit of a better quota.

Quality is thus the key to prosperity for the growers. In today's fast-growing port market, the supply keeps up with the escalating demand not by diluting the present vineyards, but by planting new ones. Even now, of the 110 million litres of wine produced in a typical year in the Douro, less than 50 million litres will be made as port. That huge surplus provides a salutary reminder of the priorities that prevail here, in a region where yields equivalent to as little as half a bottle of

Touriga Francesca is a good, deep-coloured variety, high in tannins and acidity when planted up to an altitude of 300 metres.

Tinta Barroca was introduced 50 years ago. Good for quantity as well as quality, it is well suited to blending as it has good colour, aroma and sugar content. It withstands relatively high altitudes.

74

Tinta Cão has excellent aroma and flavour but light colour. It is very much a blending variety.

Tinta Roriz ripens seven to ten days later than other varieties. With good structure and fruitiness, it makes good wine for blends. At its best at lower altitudes. It is the same variety as Spain's Tempranillo.

The Sandeman winemaking centre at
Celeirós.

wine per vine are considered quite the norm for an end product such as fine vintage port.

In common with other shippers, Sandeman has some vineyards of its own such as Quinta do Vau in the prime heartland of the Alto Douro, but buys the bulk of the grapes needed each year from independent farmers. There are more than 29,000 farmers listed in the Register through which the Casa do Douro (the viticultural arm of the Port Wine Institute) regulates production, most of them growing modest crops that would make fewer than five pipes (at 550 litres each) of port. Sandeman regularly buys from some 1,500 of these farmers, at prices that in recent years have been rising as the shippers vie for the best crops in times of increasing demand for the finest wines. To maintain the good relations that Sandeman has enjoyed for many years with the farmers the company now offers bonus payments for higher must weights (natural grape-sugar levels) in a scheme that was the first of its kind in the Douro.

The vintage itself begins in late September, with the arrival of the harvesters from the mountain villages. It is a seasonal trek that seems unlikely to be interrupted by the introduction of mechanical harvesting, as the terracing is mostly completely inaccessible to any kind of machine. Women do most of the picking, skilfully snipping away unripe or unsound fruit before dropping the bunches into their baskets. When filled, these are tipped into much larger baskets holding 100 lb (45 kilos) or more of fruit for the men to carry shoulder-high down the steep and often crumbling steps that descend as much as a dozen feet from one terrace to the next – and so on down to the lorry waiting on the road below.

The grapes are carried in capacious baskets along the narrow pathways and precipitous slopes of the vineyards to the waiting tractor-trailers or lorries on the road below.

While the methods of the pickers have changed little since the very earliest times, the pressing of the grapes has been transformed by technology. It was not until the 1960s, when hydro-electric power became available from the new Douro dams and machine crushers could be introduced, that the traditional method of treading the grapes by foot began to wane. It was a laborious business indeed, in which the fruit was tumbled into great granite troughs called *lagares*, about four feet deep and holding enough grapes to make 10,000 or more litres of wine.

A Sandeman monograph of 1889* described the treading as it had been performed for centuries:

The men, with their white pants rolled up to the mid-thigh, step into the *lagar* and form a line with their arms resting on each other's shoulders. They commence work

*Pure Port Wine, adapted from the work of writer Henry Vizetelly.

by advancing and retiring across the *lagar* with measured steps, raising and lowering their feet alternately at the word of command, 'right', 'left', as though at squad drill. As the juice exudes, and the grapes become gradually reduced to a pulp, a livelier movement follows. A fiddler, seated on the edge of the *lagar*, saws away at some merry tune, while some of the treaders join in with fife, drum, and guitar, playing and treading simultaneously.

Others swell the din with songs and shouts, intended to keep the weaker and lazier members of the gang up to their work, which is irksome and monotonous to a degree.

The first treading lasts, with occasional halts and relays of fresh men, for 18 hours or so. A long interval ensues and the treading is resumed. By this time the grapes are pretty well crushed and treading with bare feet upon the pips and stalks strewn at the bottom of the *lagar* must somewhat resemble a pilgrimage of old, when the devout trudged wearily along with hard peas packed between the soles of their feet and the soles of their shoes. The men, by this time almost dead beat, raise one purple leg after another, far into the watches of the night.

Whenever a sample of the must is wanted, the large white saucer with its convex centre is called into requisition, and one of the treaders, lifting up his brawny leg, carefully balances himself while the saucer is held to catch the must as it trickles from his dripping heel. This is inspected and tasted, and the important consideration of the amount of saccharine contained in the wine determined by means of the saccharometer. The treading completed, the must is left to ferment in the *lagar* until the saccharometer indicates that the fermentation has proceeded far enough. The stalks and skins of the grapes have formed a thick crust on the top of the must, which is then drawn off . . .

It was a picturesque business, but by the second half of the twentieth century, with the drift of so many Douro people away to the towns or better-paid work abroad, labour shortages made it a hard one to maintain. It was inevitable that the Douro would have to join the other great wine-making regions of the world in mechanising the process. The problem was to find a system that would extract the colour and flavour from the grapes with the same thoroughness and gentleness as treading does, all in the very short time that fermentation in the Douro takes to reach the critical sugar level – perhaps less than 48 hours.

Sandeman's solution was to install four of its own wine-making centres in the Douro, notably at Pacheca near Regua

'One of the treaders, lifting up his brawny leg, carefully balances himself while the saucer is held to catch the must as it trickles from his dripping heel . . .'.

and at Celeirós, further upriver not far from the little town of Pinhao, as well as at Pocinho and Riba Tua. Today in these centres, the latest autovinificators perfectly reproduce the effects of treading. Briefly, the system works like this: the grapes are unloaded into hoppers which feed into electrically driven centrifugal crushers. These strip the bunches of their stalks and crush the fruit sufficiently to break the skins without damaging the pips. (If the pips were broken they would release essential oils into the pulp, imparting bitter flavours to the wine.)

The pulp is now pumped into stainless-steel fermentation tanks which incorporate that ingenious device of the autovinificator. It works rather like a coffee percolator. The tank is filled to about three-quarters of its capacity with the pulp, or must as it is called, and sealed tight. The autovinificator system consists (in very simplified terms) of two tubes immersed in the must, with their open tops venting into a closed chamber in the top of the tank. As fermentation begins – usually through the natural action of the yeasts present in the must – carbon dioxide builds up in the air space within the tank, pressuring the must downwards. Its only escape is up one of the tubes, and into the upper chamber. Here, where the pressure is controlled by a valve system, the must is forced back down the main tube, the autovinificator itself, which sprays the must over the crust of skins that forms the *manta* on top of the liquid. The continuous process successfully imitates the laborious method by which foot-treaders kept the *manta* 'refreshed' – namely by laying boards across the *lagar* from which to reach the must, and constantly churning it up with heavy pronged paddles, or *macacos*.

As the must ferments, its natural sugar levels are repeatedly checked – they fall as the sugar is transformed into alcohol. At the usual level for port-making – between 6° and 8° on the Baumé scale – the must is ready for its union with the grape spirit which will stop the fermentation and give life to a new vintage of port.

Aguardente (literally 'firewater') is a colourless, neutral spirit of 77 per cent alcohol by volume, distilled from Portuguese grapes – not necessarily from the Douro. Wine and spirit are mixed in the proportion that has been customary for at least two centuries – four to one. Thus a pipe of port is made up of 440 litres of wine and 110 of *aguardente*. It is a crucial part of the process that the semi-fermented must and the spirit are run simultaneously into the storage vat. Wine simply added to a vat part-filled with brandy would 'burn' and take on the harsh and spiritous flavours that marred port's reputation in its earlier days.

With the must run off, the solids left behind in the fermentation tanks are pumped to presses and a further quantity of wine made, but this will not be used for the production of high-quality port.

The winemaking centre at Regua.

82

From delivery of the grapes to the fermentation process up to the blending with the spirit, the whole procedure takes just three or four days. Throughout the few weeks of the vintage, lorries arrive from the many supplying farms with the loads of grapes that keep the process going day and night. At Celeirós alone, the 50 autovinificators will produce 2 million litres of wine during the vintage.

The newly made wine stays in its vats until the New Year. The balance of wine and spirit is checked as the two elements 'marry' into a natural blend. Further brandy may be added to ensure an alcohol level sufficient to prevent any refermentation starting. The level needs to be 19% or more for this reason. Meanwhile, the lees – detritus from the fermentation – sink to the bottom of the vat and the wine 'falls bright'.

At Celeirós the wines can be overwintered in the white-domed *balão pequero* tanks that are now such a familiar sight throughout the region, or in the huge vats such as those at the Pacheca centre and lodge. Tasting during this period of the wine's infancy continues unabated as the wines are assessed for quality and character. The 'saucer' described in the 1889

Storage vats at Sandeman's Pacheca Regua winemaking centre. The lodge here is the largest in the Douro.

Top right: *Balão* storage tanks hold newly made wine over winter.

Lower right: The antique *tombladeira* tasting vessel, unique to the port trade, allows very clear examination of the wine's colour.

Overleaf: One of the bicentenary *barcos rabelos* defying parking restrictions on the forecourt of London's Guildhall.

account earlier is still very much in use as the taster's tool. It is the *tomboladeira* – a saucer indeed but with a convex centre over which wine in the rim can be shaken to allow close examination of the colour before tasting. Usually made in white porcelain to improve colour inspection, these curious-looking but indispensable vessels are unique to the port trade.

As spring approaches, the new wines are ready to be moved to the lodges in Vila Nova de Gaia. They may be transported in the pipes sent up from Sandeman's own cooperage in Oporto or by bulk carrier, and always now by road. Now that the Douro has been dammed at several points, the *barcos rabelos* no longer ply the river's once treacherous waters. (The Sandeman *rabelo* that is to be seen moored at the quayside in Gaia is a recently built replica – entirely faithful to the traditional design of these craft – which sets sail only on symbolic occasions such as the Confraria do Vinho, Porto's picturesque but vigorously competitive *rabelo* race held every 24 June to mark the city's patron saint's day. Two Sandeman *barcos rabelos* made rather lengthier voyages in the spring of 1990, one to the City of London, and another to the United States, as part of the company's bicentenary celebrations.)

The Sandeman lodges in Gaia present a modest enough facade to the harbour, but this belies the enormous storage capacity of the great galleries – all above ground – behind. Here and in further lodges such as the Barao stores, more than 10,000 pipes are held at any one time. In varying stages of

maturity, the casks lie three tiers high under dim light and in the cool, quiet conditions in which some of these wines will slumber for 5, 10, or even 20 years or more.

When the new wine arrives at the lodges, it undergoes what will be the first of many laboratory analyses in the hi-tech tasting room now located far to the rear of the building. (The original tasting room, with its stunning views over the river looking out from the first storey at the front of the lodges, is now a conference and reception area.) The taster's art is as central to the business of producing fine port as ever it was. He takes samples of all the new wines as they arrive at the lodges and assigns them to the purposes which will suit them best. One sample of the young, purple-black port might seem much the same as another to the casual visitor, but to experienced palates the characteristics that presage a wine of great quality are already detectable at this stage.

Each lot of wine is assigned to its respective Sandeman brand, for future blending with wines of other vintages to provide a consistency of style. As they mature in casks – which are marked with details of origin and date – the younger wines continue to throw lees and must be racked (drawn) off these deposits annually and transferred to fresh casks. Samples are continually taken to check the progress of the wine as the natural ageing processes mellow the purple colour to a rich ruby, then, gradually, to the coppery-brown tones of 'tawny' port.

A full-bodied ruby port such as Sandeman's Fine Ruby, a blend of wines three to four years old, is taken from lots that hold their colour and mature slowly. When ready for bottling, the wine thus has vigorous fruitiness and a vibrant ruby hue. Fine Tawny, on the other hand, while of similar age, is based on wines which mature faster, losing their colour earlier and taking on that distinctive amber-orange cast. These differing characteristics in the wine are, of course, largely determined by which grape varieties have been used and which vineyards they come from. But the fact that Douro weather conditions are so variable – particularly in very recent years – means that wines from long-established sources can alter considerably in character from one vintage to the next. The skills of the blender in sustaining consistent styles of wine are therefore constantly tested.

Premium ports such as Founders Reserve come from the same estates that provide the harvests for the great Sandeman vintage wines. Again, a number of different vintages are blended together to give a balanced wine of a consistent, recognisable style – in this case a smooth, assertively fruity port with around five to six years' cask ageing behind it, and a distinctly vintage character. Sandeman Late-Bottled Vintage, on the other hand, is a wine from the harvest of a single year, made from a blend of different wines and bottled, as the Port Wine Institute's rules dictate, during the fourth or fifth year after the vintage. The wine is made from years that are not normally declared as a vintage and, as David Sandeman has put it, 'It has something of the character of vintage port – good

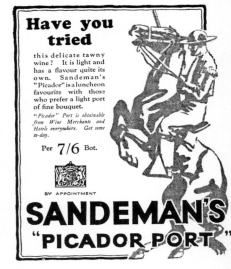

The tasting room at the Sandeman lodges, Vila Nova de Gaia. Manuel Bravo, former head taster, at work.

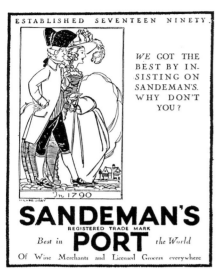

colour, good backbone . . . but Founders Reserve has a definite advantage in that in its blend we can balance by using the pick of two or three different years including a lot of declared vintage years'.

Sandeman's two aged tawny ports, Royal 10 Year Old and Imperial 20 Year Old are heirs to the wine that was for many years the firm's best-known brand, Partners' Port. Partners, first produced in 1890 to mark the House of Sandeman's centenary year and succeeded in the 1980s by Royal and Imperial, was a blend of fine wines that lost their ruby colour relatively slowly, over a period of about five years. The 10 Year Old and 20 Year Old tawnies of today are made from wines very carefully selected for their outstanding quality and colour evolution.

White port, while quite different in colour to the more richly coloured wines, is in fact produced in exactly the same way. The grapes are white (of the 51 varieties of vine permitted in the Douro, 20 bear white fruit), so the must can be steeped in the skin pulp to extract colour, flavour and tannin just as it is in the process of making the red wines. Sandeman's two white ports, Fine White and the drier Apitiv, are, like the other wines,

made from the harvests of a number of vineyards and from different vintages, blended to produce a consistent high quality and recognisable style. Many of the grapes for these wines are in fact grown in the area surrounding the firm's own wine-making centre at Celeirós.

All the ports described so far are bottled only when they are ready for drinking; they do their ageing and mellowing in cask. All these wines, indeed, are bottled at the lodges, as orders are received. (Basic wines are passed through a continuous filter immediately before bottling, and fine ports such as Founders are filtered through isothermic tanks, a very advanced chamber system which takes eight days to complete its cycle.)

Vintage port is different. It is the wine made from the best fruit in the best years – only three or four vintages out of every ten, perhaps fewer. In a 'declared' vintage, about three per cent of the total wine made will be used for the vintage port. The wines are selected by the tasters with a view to potential longevity as well as bouquet and flavour, for the final blend will be expected by knowledgeable customers to be drinking well at anything from 10 to 50 or more years thence.

The vintage wine remains two years in cask before bottling. (Recent Portuguese law has insisted on local bottling for vintage port, and all Sandeman wines are now bottled at the lodges.) The maturing of the wine therefore largely takes place in glass. This means the colour does not take on the tawny cast it would in wood. It means, too, that the deposit thrown in the ageing process will remain in the wine, gradually accumulating as a 'crust' on the bottle's inner undersurface as it lies in the cellar. According to the conditions prevailing during the harvest in question, some vintages will take longer to come round than others. The amount of tannin naturally present in the grape skins is a major factor. A high tannin extract means that Sandeman's 1977 vintage will last well into the next century – its fruit kept vibrantly alive by this natural preservative. A vintage such as 1975, on the other hand, with a lower tannin extract, is a comparative lightweight – delicious to drink only ten years after the vintage, but not a wine for long keeping.

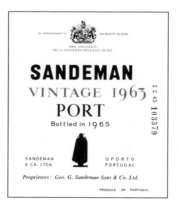

The decision to declare a vintage must be taken while the wine is still in cask. Because the wines of each shipper, and the opinions of each shipper's tasters, vary considerably there is rarely a universal declaration. Sandeman's great 1797 vintage, said to be among the best ports ever made, was in fact from a year officially condemned as 'very bad, tawny'. Likewise, the classic Sandeman 1911, the Coronation Vintage that marked the enthronement of George V, was not even declared by any other British shipper.

While the experience of the taster is invaluable in assessing the prospects of the port in cask, it is impossible to predict with any certainty how any given vintage will turn out in the end. As an entirely natural wine, the port evolves through the processes dictated by nature, just as those first Sandeman vintages of the 1790s did, and just as great vintage port surely always will.

Chapter IX

Sandeman in Jerez – the Nineteenth Century

In the early 1800s, sherry enjoyed a well-established but modest following in Britain. Imports averaged, as they had done for much of the preceding century, a little under 10,000 butts (each equivalent to 54 cases) a year. Ahead, in the 1840s to the 1870s, lay the dramatic boom triggered by Victorian society's adoption of sherry. In the meantime, the Jerez trade formed a relatively minor part of Sandeman's business.

The firm began the new century as London agents for one of the great figures of the sherry trade, James Duff. British consul in Cadiz for 25 years until his death, aged 81, in 1815, Duff had been a shipper at least since the 1760s, perhaps longer. George Sandeman may well have established the connection with him in person during his early travels in Spain. Fellow Scots, they were clearly on amicable terms. A letter to George from his father, welcoming him back from his travels in 1802, acknowledges his son's news that he had had 'the good fortune just to be in time to shake hands with your steady and good friend Mr Duff on his immediate setting out for Cadiz'.

James Duff's reputation as a gentleman and a diplomat – he was knighted for his consular services during the Peninsular War – was well matched by his good name as a sherry shipper. Sandeman offered London customers no less than eight different classes of sherry, as well as other wines from the region that are less familiar today. One was Paxarete, a sweet, liquorous wine made from Pedro Ximenez grapes grown at Prado del Rey about 60 km north-east of Jerez. Paxarete was a dark wine used mostly even in those days to give colour to paler sherries. But it was valued as a drink in its own right, and priced accordingly – £31 10s a butt, compared to £25 10s for ten-year-old sherry. Also listed was a wine that is now all but extinct, Rota Tent. This was red wine ('tent' is a corruption of the Spanish *tinto* for red wine) from the village of Rota on the coast between Sanlucar and Puerto de Santa Maria. Made from the black-skinned Tintilla grape, it was a dryish, intense, fortified wine intended for very long ageing. Sandeman were offering it at £9 a hogshead (half the size of a butt) in 1800.

Sandeman continued to act as Duff's London agents until 1805, when the shipper ended the arrangement in favour of his nephew, Sir William Duff Gordon, whom he wished to encourage into the sherry trade. Sir William succeeded his uncle in 1815 at the head of the firm that was to become, under his name, one of the most renowned of all shippers.

In the meantime, Sandeman wasted no time in finding new agency business. By August 1805, they were representing another important shipper of the day, W. Lacoste & Lagarde. It was in that month that Sandeman's sent out their famous circular to customers, exhorting them to take advantage of a

'Convoy now going out to Portugal' and assure their deliveries of port and sherry. That convoy was, of course, part of the fleet that was destined for Trafalgar.

Sherry sales boomed in the wake of the great victory, and by 1809 George Sandeman had decided it was time to enter the trade more directly. He sent his partner James Gooden to Spain to establish an office in Cadiz and ship wines under the Sandeman name. A circular of April 1809 announced the new business:

El Corregidor from the air.

From the white *albariza* soil at El Corregidor come the palomino grapes to make the finest *oloroso* sherry.

We beg leave to acquaint you, that we continue to forward orders for ... Sherries, to our partner, Mr Gooden, now at Cadiz, and that every exertion will be made under existing circumstances, to execute them to your satisfaction.

Unfortunately, under the circumstances that did exist at the time, even Mr Gooden's exertions were not, in the beginning at least, to prove equal to the task. In 1810, war between Spain and Napoleon brought French armies to Andalusia. Jerez was captured, and Cadiz besieged. The sherry trade was forced into a limbo that lasted until late in 1812 when the French withdrew north – leaving the vineyards and *bodegas* in ruins.

As trade resumed, Sandeman revived the connection with the Duff family. The firm was certainly representing Duff Gordon shortly after Sir James Duff's death late in 1815, and may have been doing so earlier. Gordon, Murphy & Co., the company set up by Sir William Duff Gordon back in 1805 to handle his uncle's wines, had prospered greatly, thanks largely to the efforts of its manager, John James Ruskin. Then, in 1814, Ruskin left to join Pedro Domecq in the firm that was to make his fortune – and, incidentally, to provide the inheritance that helped his son John Ruskin to become the Victorian Age's greatest aesthete.

The fortunes of Gordon, Murphy & Co. meanwhile declined and the company collapsed in 1820. While the name Duff Gordon can hardly have been enhanced by this regrettable demise – widely rumoured to have been accelerated by the prodigal habits of the Gordon, Murphy partners – the reputation of the house's sherries was never in question. Duff Gordon's substantial sales through Sandeman provided what Julian Jeffs in his book *Sherry* called 'a reliable connexion that greatly helped matters'. By 1818, Duff Gordon wines were fetching higher prices than those of any other shipper.

It was in 1818 that Julian Pemartin founded his sherry business. Four years later, Sandeman became the agents for the new firm and, ultimately, its owners. Early documents suggest that Pemartin, from an émigré French family, had established himself as a merchant specialising in trade with North African countries in the previous century. Correspondence with one

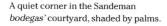

A quiet corner in the Sandeman *bodegas'* courtyard, shaded by palms.

SHIPPD, by the Grace of God, in Good Order and well-conditioned, by *Cemartin & Co*
in and upon the good Ship called the *Amelia* Jn *Bulley*
whereof is Master, under God, for this present Voyage
and now riding at Anchor in the *Bay of Cadiz* and by God's Grace bound for
to say
Hull & Leith

Four Butts of Sherry Wine

Y Nº 3 — 2 Butts
— 4 — 2 d
4 Butts

being marked and numbered as in the Margin, and are to be delivered in the like good Order and well-conditioned, at the aforesaid Port of *Hull* (The Act of God, the King's Enemies, Fire, and all and every other Danger and Accidents of the Seas, Rivers, and Navigation, of whatever Nature and Kind soever excepted) unto *Sam Younger & Co of Sheffield*
or to their Assigns, he or they paying Freight for the said Goods *Seven Pounds Sterling & 10 pe Primage*
with Primage and Average accustomed. In witness whereof the said Master or Purser of the said Ship hath affirmed to 4 Bills of Lading, all of this Tenor and Date, the one of which Bills being accomplished, the other 3 to stand void. And so God send the good Ship to her desired Port in Safety. Amen. Dated in *Cadiz 2nd Decbr 1822*.
Contents unknown not accountable for leakage

John Bulley

SHIPPED, by the Grace of God, in Good Order and well-conditioned, by *Pemartin & Co*
in and upon the good Ship called the *Phylcca*
whereof is Master, under God, for this present Voyage, *Christopher Hill*
and now riding at Anchor in the *Bay of Cadiz* and by God's Grace bound for
London to say

Twenty five Butts & Twenty five Hogsheads of Sherry Wine

20. Butts 20. Hhds
5 — 5 —
25. Butts 25. Hhds.

being marked and numbered as in the Margin, and are to be delivered in the like good Order and well-conditioned, at the aforesaid Port of *London* (The Act of God, the King's Enemies, Fire, and all and every other Danger and Accidents of the Seas, Rivers, and Navigation, of whatever Nature and Kind soever excepted) unto *Messrs Sandeman Gooden & Forster*
or to their Assigns, he or they paying Freight for the said Goods *Forty eight Pounds two Shillings Sixpence St & 10 pe Cent Primage*
with Primage and Average accustomed. In witness whereof the said Master or Purser of the said Ship hath affirmed to four Bills of Lading, all of this Tenor and Date; the one of which four Bills being accomplished, the other three to stand void. And so God send the good Ship to her desired Port in Safety. Amen. Dated in *Cadiz 3 April 1824*.
Contents unknown & not Accountable for Leakage

Christ Hill

SHIPPED, by the Grace of God, in Good Order and well-conditioned, by *Pemartin & Co*
in and upon the good Ship called the *Pearthingwell* Wm *Chapman*
whereof is Master, under God, for this present Voyage
and now riding at Anchor in the *Bay of Cadiz* and by God's Grace, bound for
Southampton & Hull to say

Three Butts & two Hhds of Sherry Wine

GS Nº 3 — 1 Butt 2 Hhds
" — 4 — 1 d
" — 5 — 1 d
3 Butts 2 Hhds

being marked and numbered as in the Margin, and are to be delivered in the like good Order and well-conditioned, at the aforesaid Port of *Hull* (The Act of God, the King's Enemies, Fire, and all and every other Danger and Accidents of the Seas, Rivers, and Navigation, of whatever Nature and Kind soever excepted) unto *Messrs Geo: Mansfield & Co*
or to their Assigns, he or they paying Freight for the said Goods *Seven Pounds Sterling & 10 pe Primage*
with Primage and Average accustomed. In witness whereof the said Master or Purser of the said Ship hath affirmed to 4 Bills of Lading, all of this Tenor and Date; the one of which Bills being accomplished, the other 3 to stand void. And so God send the good Ship to her desired Port in Safety. Amen. Dated in *Cadiz 7 June 1822*.
Contents unknown not accountable for leakage

Wm Chapman

Early bills of lading for sherry shipped by Pemartin & Co.

Pedro Duval hints darkly at involvement in the slave trade, but Pemartin may not have been actively concerned in it.

Whatever his past activities were, Pemartin made rapid progress as a sherry shipper. In 1822, their first year as his agents, Sandeman offered no less than six different Pemartin wines. New wine was priced at £28 per butt on board at Cadiz while the best 'very superior old' cost £53. By 1836 Pemartin & Co. were among the top ten shippers, with exports for that year of 1,154 butts. Twenty years later, with the British market now burgeoning, Pemartin sales were 3,239 butts – more even than Domecq and Duff Gordon.

In 1853, Julian Pemartin died, leaving his business to his three sons, Julian, José and Francisco. Julian junior is the subject of a favourite Sandeman story that well illustrates the cultural divide between conservative Spain and liberal Britain of those times. When George Sandeman suggested, in 1829, that young Julian might benefit from the experience of working awhile at Sandeman's London office, his aunt was scandalised. 'That *Babylon*' she hissed. (It is assumed she referred to London in general rather than to 20 St Swithin's Lane in particular.)

The younger Julian's protective upbringing does not appear to have saved him entirely from temptation, because soon after he and his brothers assumed control of Pemartin & Co. they were running into difficulties with money. Julian's extravagant lifestyle, ultimately expressed by the extraordinary *grand siècle* palace he had built for himself in Jerez, caused him frequently to ask for advances from Sandeman. Julian's brothers wrote personally to George Glas Sandeman in 1864:

> You will see by our letter to the firm that we have drawn £3,000 on you though we had written that we would cease drawing any more till we heard from you on the subject.
> Unforeseen circumstances have obliged us to do so...

The quality of Pemartin wines, meanwhile, was suffering. George Glas Sandeman wrote to Julian, also in 1864:

> I am sorry to find complaints on all hands about the shipments you are now making. It appears then that your late purchases for the Soleras are spoiling them as your Nos. 1, 2, 3 etc are all so deteriorated that it is impossible to make way with them. I also find that our taste and comparison on this side do not agree with your report upon them – I think it therefore safer to refuse orders than to lose connexions by executing them.

At the end of 1866, Julian Pemartin dissolved the partnership he had formed with his brothers on their father's death, resolving to carry on the business alone. George Glas Sandeman was unimpressed, coolly informing Julian that he and his brothers were so little known amongst Sandeman's customers that there would be no point in announcing the dissolution. He went on, in a letter of December 1866, to give Pemartin his opinion about the way business was going:

For the last few years, we have been convinced the business cannot be productive to you or us as it is. The latitude given to your employees to have bodegas, and sell to you, and buy for you, are abuses that always increase, and it is in vain for you or for us to attempt to make our connexions pay while your competitors manage their business so much better, and undersell you. It is quite out of the question our getting from our connexions the enormous prices of your invoices, for such wines as the No. 1, 2 and 3 and GGS/P – even the last mark, which we have been in the habit of using at our own tables, we cannot drink and the price is £82!

In fairness to Pemartin, prices had been rising throughout the trade. The fungal pest oidium had attacked the Jerez vineyards in the 1850s and there were outbreaks of another insect infestation that wrecked all the harvests of the late 1860s. By now, the demand for sherry was five times what it had been at the beginning of the century. Shippers were under pressure, and quality was bound to slip. Prices meanwhile doubled for new wines from the depleted harvests of 1855 to 1870.

But Pemartin brought difficulties of his own on himself. He bought wine in from *almacenistas* – speculators who purchased at low cost from large harvests and then waited for shortfalls and high prices in subsequent years – some of whom were actually on his payroll. George Glas Sandeman warned him against these 'middle men' and the danger they posed to his business: 'When you allow those you employ to be Almacenistas, the fortunes you enable them to acquire prevent your meeting the competition of your rivals.'

Privately, Pemartin's improvidence was following suit. In 1865, Sandeman agent John Nicoll visited Jerez and mentioned in a letter home that Julian had 'begun to build a fine large house (according to the plans) just outside Jerez'. Pemartin's monumental folly, this was the El Recreo de las Cadenas, a palatial house designed by Charles Garnier, architect of the Opéra in Paris. It is a mark of Julian Pemartin's charm, not to

Above left: Julian Pemartin's extravagant *palacio* became a Sandeman property in 1879.

96

El Corregidor Vineyard.

mention his social connections, that he managed to persuade Garnier to work on this outlandish project at all. The house was duly completed in 1870 – in the same nostalgic Louis XIV style as the Opéra, and five years earlier than the great theatre itself.

In the finely proportioned rooms of his vast new residence, Pemartin entertained on a lavish scale. He was undaunted, it seems, by the fact that the year in which he took possession of the palace saw him declared insolvent. From 1870 his business was run under the direction of a *Junta Directiva* nominated by his creditors. The fact that this council of Jerez worthies included Julian Pemartin himself among its members may well account for the fact that his extravagances continued unabated for the rest of the decade.

Even though the sherry market was flourishing, and the vintages of the 1870s showed great improvements, Pemartin still had troubles of his own. His other businesses, including banking, did not fare consistently well, and he was unlucky enough to become embroiled in the political upheavals of the

97

time when a republican mob looted and wrecked his *bodega* in 1871.

In 1879, Pemartin was bankrupted. As Julian Jeffs tells it, he went out in style, throwing a great ball at the Jerez palace for the King of Spain, who complimented his host amidst the festivities on the completeness of his hospitality.

'Your Majesty is mistaken,' Pemartin replied. 'One thing is missing: a rope to hang myself with, for I am a ruined man.'

On 31 October 1879, the business was liquidated. Sandeman, following negotiations that had in fact begun in the previous year, took over all of Pemartin's assets – vineyards, *bodegas*, all the stocks of wine, the shipping business complete. Also included was the palace.

The deal, which discharged his enormous debts to Sandeman (they had reached £10,000 by 1876) did not leave Pemartin entirely destitute, as he retained possession of the sherry brands that bore his name. Sandeman paid a rental and royalties for their use. In 1889, the brands became Sandeman's absolute property under an agreement with Julian Pemartin's heirs (he had died childless in 1884, leaving his remaining interest to two nephews).

Thus, 70 years after first briefly shipping sherry under the Sandeman name, the firm was back in the business. Again, however, it was not an entirely auspicious time at which to have done so. The 1870s brought a rash of reports in the British press that drink in general and sherry in particular were injurious to the health of both body and soul. Doctors wrote, erroneously, of the dangers posed by the gypsum and sulphur used in the sherry-making process. Rumours were spread that

Traditional, laborious pressing at El Corregidor. The *lagares* here are the last remaining in Jerez and are used every year to produce a small quantity of sherry as part of the harvest *fiesta* celebrations.

The courtyard at Cerro Viejo.

sherry caused gout. William Booth's Salvation Army, formally militarised in 1878, added to the growing chorus for temperance.

Sherry did, admittedly, present a high-profile target. The boom of the last half-century had institutionalised it as the favourite wine of the Victorian middle class. In the 1870s, it accounted for more than 40 per cent of all the wine drunk in Britain. It was commonly served throughout meals. (The 'aperitif' hour was as yet still unheard-of.) The poor harvests of the 1850s and 1860s had led, however, to inferior wines finding their way onto the market. And the high prices had lured wine fraudsters into the business. 'Sherry' began to appear from some very unlikely sources, not just elsewhere in Spain, but from Germany and even France. Australia, South Africa and North America soon joined in.

Sherry's enemies had a field day, but the wine did have its stalwart defenders – outside the trade as well as within it. One such was the journalist Henry Vizetelly, who set out to investigate the allegations made about the wine. He spent several months in Jerez, and published his findings in a seminal book of 1876, *Facts about Sherry*. His visit to the Sandeman properties, fully reported in the book, and later adapted as an essay, provides an excellent account of the firm's shipping business in its earliest times:

> A thoroughly typical Jerez shipping establishment is that of Messrs Sandeman, Buck & Co., the successors of the old-established and historical house of Pemartin, whose extensive premises and stock of rare old wines, together

The Calle Pizarro entrance to the Bodega Grande, around 1910. (This *bodega* was burnt to the ground in 1912 but quickly rebuilt.) The train transported the casks direct from the *bodegas* to the Cadiz docks.

Overleaf: The Sandeman *bodegas* at the turn of the century.

Storks have nested each year at Sandeman in Jerez for generations, returning every February from their African winter quarters to breed atop the chimney high above the *bodegas*.

100

Sandeman

102

with the stately Louis Quatorze palace in the midst of charming gardens, erected by Señor Julian Pemartin, were acquired by the existing firm a few years back. The establishment comprises, in addition to bodegas and offices, which form two large separate blocks, accessible from four streets, a cooperage, and various supplementary workshops, so that the process of cask-making and seasoning, and the rearing, blending and shipping of wine can here be followed from beginning to end. Access is gained through one of the bodegas to a pleasant court, planted with orange and acacia trees, and having a picturesque dome-roofed structure in its centre. Here are the offices, where the chances are that wine-brokers with samples will be waiting for an interview with one of the principals, while a group of wine-growers who have sold their vintages to the firm are taking their turn at the cashier's desk to be paid. Hard by is the shipping sample room, stocked with bottles containing samples of all the export orders executed by the house, each with a label setting forth the exact composition of the blend and the date when the wine was shipped. Hence, whenever an order is repeated, the sample embraces it to be reproduced with the same scrupulous exactitude as a photograph can be reproduced from the original negative.

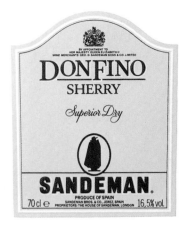

Inside the bodegas the light is carefully mellowed, whilst the air is redolent with the aromatic perfume of wine. Along their lofty aisles, divided by arches of masonry, are ranged countless butts, with mystic signs chalked on their heads denoting their contents to the initiated – the 'palm-leaf' of the developing amontillados, the 'cut stick' of the future oloroso, and the perpendicular lines of the single, double, and triple 'rayas' (differing grades of grape must). Moving briskly about are groups of 'arrumbadores' or cellarmen – sturdy fellows, looking as though unlimited Sherry certainly agreed with them, nattily dressed in coloured shirts, light pants, and gay crimson sashes. Some are drawing off wine for shipment in iron-bound wooden pitchers, called 'jarras' while others are laboriously hoisting butts into position on the upper tiers by means of sloping skids and ropes.

If the bodegas and even the butts have a family resemblance, there is a marked difference as regards the contents of some of the latter. The pride and boast of the firm are wines of the true old Sherry type – so justly high in favour before a taste for paler and too often inferior varieties set in – some of the soleras of which date back to the year 1818, and have never been 'refreshed' by aught save wine selected from growths of the best vineyards around Jerez. In butts blackened with age are venerable wines of this class, concentrated by time, very deep in colour, full and pungent in taste, and powerful in aroma – too potent in flavour, in fact, for ordinary drinking, but invaluable for blending purposes. There are also other deep and full-bodied, well-rounded Jerezano wines,

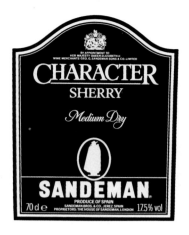

bright, generous, and robust, of nutty flavour, ample roundness and rich aroma, carrying their thirty or forty years buoyantly, together with amber-tinted growths of refined flavour and great vinosity.

Vizetelly's enthusiasm may well have been caught from his hosts of that time, for Albert George Sandeman, who had succeeded his father as head of the firm in 1868, was strongly committed to the sherry business. He appointed as the Jerez manager Walter J. Buck, who became a partner in the new business from its formation in 1879. Buck was recruited from the firm of Matthieson, Furlong, with which Sandeman had had dealings in the 1870s, and was one of the great sherry-makers of his day. He remained in charge of the Jerez business until his death in 1917.

The 1890s brought two very significant developments. The first was the unwelcome arrival in the Jerez vineyards of the phylloxera in 1894. As had already happened throughout Europe, the vines were devastated. By now, the practice of replanting with phylloxera-resistant American rootstocks was established, so there was a measure of damage control in the vineyards, but harvests were seriously affected nonetheless.

The second development was Sandeman's response to the peril that the prospect of a series of short vintages presented – namely the interruption of the flow of wines through the *soleras*. In spite of the falling market for sherry at the time, Sandeman decided to invest for the future and persuaded the grower Don Antonio Bernaldo de Quirós to sell them his entire stock of *añadas* – unblended wines of individual vintages – made between 1872 and 1882 at his Carrascal vineyard. Today, it is not easy to convey the boost that this demonstration of faith in its future gave to sherry, but it was a huge purchase of rare wines – 800 casks – by a firm whose head, Albert Sandeman, was not unknown as a shrewd investor (he was appointed Governor of the Bank of England in the following year). A report of the sale quoted in *The Times* of 18 April 1894 put it like this:

> The disposal of these Añadas of genuine and unique character collected for so many years from his vineyard by Don Antonio Bernaldo de Quirós, and left to mature, each cask by itself pure and unblended, in the old-fashioned way, has made the sale of this historical Bodega a matter of sensation in our market. At the present time no such parcel exists in the hands of Almacenistas. The sale has had the effect of strengthening a belief in the future of fine sherry.

It was from this outstanding collection of wines that Albert George Sandeman selected a series of casks that provided the basis for the Sandeman Rare Sherries available in the 1990s. Royal Ambrosante, for example, comes from a *solera* established with 12 casks selected in 1897, and since carefully built up to 18. Imperial Corregidor, the rich *oloroso* derived exclusively from Sandeman's El Corregidor vineyard at the heart of the Carrascal district, was first selected in 1895.

Sandeman

These wines, described by Julian Jeffs as 'to sherry what the first growth clarets are to Bordeaux', are a mark of the supreme quality of which sherry is capable. And a mark, too, of the fact that Sandeman will be starting the next century in Jerez with every bit as much confidence as it did the twentieth.

Courtyard at El Corrigedor

Chapter X

Sherry – the Making of the Wine

The Jerez vineyards lie on the gently undulating hills that surround the city, between 30 and 150 metres above sea level, and all within a radius of about 20 miles. In summer, this is a parched landscape, without rainfall from June to September. Temperatures routinely rise to 38°C (100°F), baking the fields of sunflowers and sugar beet to a brittle brown, and bringing clouds of dust into the air in the wake of the few vehicles to be seen venturing along the ill-made roads that thread the hills.

Emerging from the bleak suburban sprawl of the city into this cauldron would be forbidding indeed were it not for the great swathes of lush green that the vineyards superimpose on the arid backdrop. Only vines – with a lifespan of 30 years or more – have the tenacity to survive here. Their short, gnarled stems belie the metres of roots that seek out the water far underground – absorbed during the winter rains through the stark, white chalk that passes for topsoil. This *albariza* ground, composed 80 per cent of chalk with the remainder magnesium and clay, is much the best medium for grape-growing here – particularly for *finos*, the palest, lightest and driest of sherries. *Barro* (clay) and *arena* (sand) are graded as lower-quality soils. Of the Sandeman vineyards, more than two-thirds lie in *albariza*.

The most prized districts lie to the north-west of Jerez. At Macharnudo, Sandeman have six vineyards: Cerro Viejo (where the company's winemaking centre stands), La Loba, Santa Teresa, Santa Emilia, La Palma and San Isidro. Carrascal, east of Macharnudo, is famous for the fragrant *oloroso* wines, and includes Sandeman's great El Corregidor vineyard plus two others, El Castillo and San Miguel.

More than 90 per cent of the vines grown in the sherry zone are of the Palomino Fino variety, an indigenous plant named not as might be expected in connection with the local equestrian tradition, but after a thirteenth-century nobleman. The Palomino is grown elsewhere in Spain, and farther afield, but only in Jerez does it aspire to greatness, producing sizeable yields of high-quality white grapes in the large, loosely packed bunches that commonly have to be propped to prevent them trailing on the ground.

There is only one other principal variety, the Pedro Ximenez, also bearing white grapes. The name is a translation of Peter Siemens, the German soldier said to have first brought this variety to Spain from the Rhine during the Hundred Years War, six centuries ago. The PX, as the vine is universally known, used to be very much more widely planted than it is today, and is progressively giving way to the Palomino. PX grapes provide

Overleaf: The weight of the bunches draws the fruit almost down to the ground. Picking is largely a low-level task.

the concentrated sweet and dark juice for enriching natural sherries – which are otherwise entirely dry wines.

Most wines are nowadays planted along rows up to about two metres apart, to allow for mechanised cultivation. The trunks of the vines are short – not much more than 40 cm – and pruned so that only four branches are allowed to grow. Of these, two in turn are permitted to produce fruit in alternate years. They are trailed along stout wires to support the bunches.

Until recently, mildew was a major problem in the vineyards most years. It attacked the underside of the vine leaves during the damp spring, withering them and depriving the new fruit of shade from the sun. The cure lies in spraying with a copper sulphate solution, but during a sudden outbreak even a large team of sprayers cannot hope to reach all the vines in time. In bad years, a third of the entire crop might be lost. Today, the spraying is done by tractor, covering an entire vineyard in hours, so it coats both the upper and lower surfaces of the leaves. It makes a dramatic difference to the vines'

productivity. Vines on *albariza* that once yielded less than two kilos of fruit each can now produce nearly three kilos.

Vine and soil are wholly complementary. The Palomino and Pedro Ximenez vines alike produce true sherry only in the geological conditions that prevail in the Jerez vineyards, as defined by the *Consejo Regulador*, the Controlling Council for Sherry.

Traditionally, the vintage starts on 10 September, but may start as early as the third week in August, according to weather conditions. When the grapes are fully ripe, the vintagers lop off the bunches and place them in baskets or, more usually today, rigid crates, for loading on to the lorry or tractor that will carry the fruit to the press house.

To concentrate the juice in the Pedro Ximenez grapes, the bunches are laid out in the sun – for two or more weeks. This long exposure for PX shrivels the grapes almost to raisins so that they produce a dense and supersweet juice. To allow for the long period of sunning, PX grapes are picked before Palomino, and pressed after.

All the wines needed for the annual Sandeman vintage are now made at the Cerro Viejo centre, where modern horizontal presses and 100 fermentation vats produce high-quality results in controlled conditions. But it was not always so. In earlier times, the grapes would be pressed at several different vineyard press houses by very much less sophisticated means.

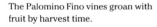
The Palomino Fino vines groan with fruit by harvest time.

In the traditional pressing, the grapes were piled into *lagares*, wooden treading boxes raised on trestles, with sides just about knee height and about five metres square – large enough to hold more than half a ton of fruit. Men wearing rawhide boots, with nails driven in at acute angles for crushing the grapes

without splitting the pips open, then tramped up and down in a long and laborious ritual. The juice ran down the obliquely angled floor of the trough and out through a sieve into a collecting tub. It was then ladled, via another sieve, into casks.

According to the type of sherry to be made, the 'free-run' juice from the treading might be used separately from the juice produced in the second phase of the pressing – in which the pulp was crushed by a hand-turned screw to extract the last of the liquid. Where all the juice was to be used together, the capacity of one *lagar* – about 700 kilos of fruit – would fill a 600 litre *bodega* butt, leaving space to allow for bubbling during the forthcoming fermentation.

This picturesque method is now almost extinct, although a few butts are still made – with due ceremony – in the lovingly preserved press house at El Corregidor. The old *lagares* there are the last working examples left in any of the Jerez vineyards.

Another ancient practice in sherry-making is the addition of *yeso* – plaster – to the grapes immediately before treading or pressing. In vintages where the grapes are very ripe, there is the danger that the natural sugar content will be too high and the acidity too low. Adding a small quantity of gypsum – in fact calcium sulphate – corrects the acidity and also aids clarification of the wine. It is an entirely safe process, and the quasi-medical furore that broke out over it in the latter part of the last century had no real substance whatsoever.

More exact methods of controlling acidity and improving clarification have since entirely displaced the use of gypsum. Likewise, the whole business of extracting the juice has

Harvest days are long and arduous.

changed beyond recognition. Grapes are fed by a moving screw into a centrifugal machine which gently separates the stalks from the fruit and breaks the skins. The crushed grapes pass through decanting vats, where their own weight is enough to open them and create a flow of juice, or 'must'. This free-run must accounts for about three-quarters of the yield. For the final pressing the pulp is passed on to a perforated drum and the must expelled through slits just too small to admit the pips and skins. Control of pressure is exact, and a clearer juice is obtained than would ever be possible from treading.

The must is now run into fermentation vats in a complex of four *bodegas* especially built for the purpose at Cerro Viejo. Within hours the must is bubbling and frothing inside the casks or vats. This is the 'tumultous fermentation' prompted by the yeasts naturally present on the fruit and in the warm late-summer air. This fermentation lasts three or four days before subsiding into the gentler secondary one. During this – which lasts for a period of about ten weeks – every vestige of sugar is converted into alcohol and the grape juice evolves into a completely dry wine with an alcoholic strength of 11 or 12 per cent by volume.

Distinct from this dry wine are two other quite different types. Pedro Ximenez (PX) from the grapes of the same name is ultra-sweet, pressed from the raisin-like grapes and so concentrated with natural sugar that the must cannot fully ferment. (Fermentation is controlled by adding a little grape spirit.) The finished wine has a sweetness measure on the Beaumé scale of 23° or 24° – much too sweet to drink as a

straight sherry, but perfect as a blending wine to sweeten full-bodied sherries.

Dulce is another non-dry wine. It is made from Palomino grapes, usually from *barro* or *arena* soils or from an *albariza* vineyard too recently planted to yield a first-class conventional sherry. The grapes are not sunned in the way of PX, but a larger dose of alcohol is added to arrest fermentation, producing a wine of 8° sweetness on the Baumé scale. *Dulce* is ideal for blending light and medium sherries whose delicacy might be overwhelmed by PX.

Towards the end of February, the fermentation long over, the young wines are ready for inspection. The *bodega* manager and his *capataz* – the head foreman – at this stage take note of the characteristics of the good wines, and reject the not so good.

The grapes are fed by a moving screw into a centrifugal machine which gently separates the stalks from the fruit and breaks the skins.

A skilled *venenciador* can fill a handful of narrow-mouthed *copita* glasses without spilling a single drop.

114

Fresh-drawn *fino* sherry. The glass on the right clearly shows the *flor*.

Wine from casks is still examined with the aid of the *venencia*, a deep and narrow silver cup attached to the end of a metre-long, flexible handle. The *venenciador* dips the cup through the bung hole in the top of the cask, deep into the wine. Holding the handle about halfway up, he then raises the cup aloft in one smooth movement, cascading the contents into the glass – or even several glasses – he holds in his other hand, without spilling a drop. Their awesome skills have made *venenciadors* media stars in their own right in recent years, with Sandeman's brilliant Juan Galindo and Vicente Sanchez Garcia among the best known of all.

The timeless skills of every member of the *bodega* workforce are tested to the full as the yearly process of selecting wine for the continuous sherry process starts once more. The tasters examine the colour and nose of the new wines – which are aerated, accentuating their aromas, by the *venenciador*'s long-distance pouring – holding the *catavino* tasting glass up to the light. Since the completion of fermentation, the wine has been 'falling bright', clarifying as the detritus of the ferments settle to the bottom of the cask. From the approved casks, samples are taken and tested for alcoholic strength, acidity and other natural characteristics.

Wines that pass muster in the laboratory are now racked off the lees (gently siphoned out of the cask without disturbing the lees or deposit, on the cask's bottom) and fortified with wine alcohol. This alcohol is an equal mixture of grape spirit and mature sherry, as adding pure spirit to the young wine could cause harm to it. At this stage, the fortification brings the alcohol level up from the post-fermentation 11 or 12 per cent to 15 or 15.5 per cent alcohol by volume. It now passes into fresh

The *venenciador* at work in the *bodegas*.

117

casks, to develop in *añadas*, rows of casks classified by year and vineyard. Here each cask of dry sherry will imperceptibly develop its own style – and it will be at least another year before that style can be classified with any certainty.

This stage of the wine's development is one of the unsolved mysteries of sherry – arguably as much of an enigma to today's scientifically minded experts as it was to the first Sandemans in the 1790s. It is still common to find three neighbouring *añada* casks of wine from the same vineyard, pressed, fermented and racked together, under identical conditions, producing three quite distinct types of sherry.

What determines the difference is the variation in the yeasts that predominate, apparently randomly, in each cask. One of these yeasts is the source of another of the mysteries that make sherry such a unique wine: the *flor del vino*, the flower of the wine. A few months after the fermentation, just at the time the vines out in the vineyards are flowering, the *flor* appears as a white film over the surface of the wine. Feeding on the oxygen in the airspace between the wine and the loosely bunged top of the cask, the *flor* can grow to a thick crust that rather resembles clouds viewed from an aircraft far above. It is to encourage this strange phenomenon that 600-litre casks are filled only 500 litres full. Air, of course, is hazardous to wine, but the *flor* keeps the oxygen out; the fortification of the wine, meanwhile, protects the *flor* from the harmful effects of the microbes that inevitably collect in the airspace. It is a mutually beneficent alliance in every way except that the airiness in cask does mean high evaporation – as much as 4 per cent a year. But the cost is fully compensated for: it is the *flor* that gives so much sherry its extraordinary flavour.

In the late spring, the *flor* disintegrates and falls to the bottom of the cask. There it forms the crust known as the *madre del vino*, mother of the wine, which is left undisturbed. As autumn approaches, the *flor* will appear once more – to die again in the winter. But this cycle would not continue throughout a second year if the wine simply remained in its original cask. The *flor* needs a constant supply of fresh wine to feed on, allowing it to continue to work its magic on the sherry as it develops over at least three years. (This is the minimum period, as defined under Spain's wine laws. In practice, sherry develops for at least four years.)

Display cask in the visitor reception area at the Sandeman *bodegas* shows the *flor* atop the *fino* sherry.

The need for constant 'refreshing' of the developing wines with those of subsequent vintages has created sherry's famous *solera* system. All sherry is made by the system, and in Sandeman's *bodegas* the series of casks that give the system its name include several that date back to the last century.

It can all seem bewilderingly complicated, and is best explained by starting with the wines of the new vintage as they are brought from Cerro Viejo to join the *soleras* in the vast, cathedral-like Sandeman *bodegas* in Jerez. The *añada* casks from the new harvest are classified into four main styles by the team of experts. First, there are the *finos*, the lightest, both in colour and body, making a dry and fresh wine in bottle such as Sandeman's Don Fino from a long established *solera*. Second,

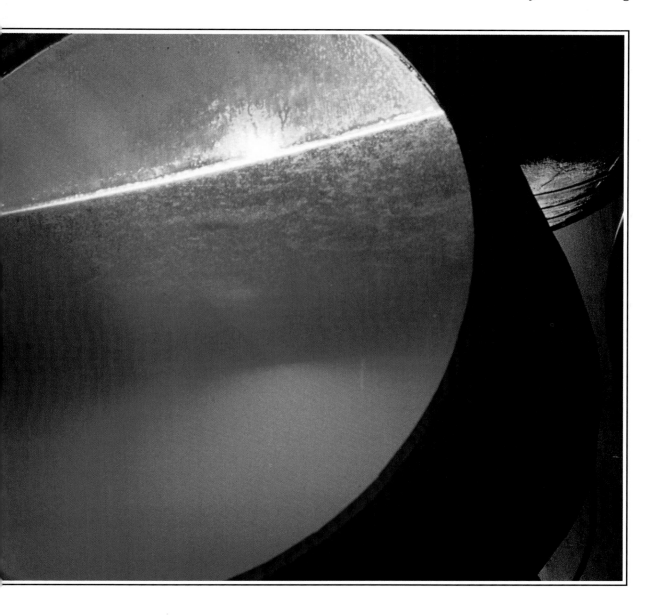

there are the *amontillados*, fuller-bodied and tending with age to take on more colour than the *finos*. They are naturally dry, but a little PX or *dulce* is often blended with them to give a medium-dry character marked by a hazelnutty flavour – Sandeman Medium Dry is a classic example. Third, there are *olorosos*, very full-bodied and attaining a rich golden colour. When blended with PX these otherwise dry wines are known as Cream Sherries, thus the name for Sandeman's fragrant and luscious Armada Cream. (Some *olorosos* of less finesse are classified as *rayas* and are used for blending.) Finally, there is the rarest style of sherry, the *palo cortado*, which can be loosely described as something between an *amontillado* and an *oloroso*. Sandeman Dry Old Palo Cortado is one of the few authentic wines of this style made today.

Once classified, sherries are grouped in fresh casks by type, no longer by year, and are matured in their respective systems. It helps to explain that the word *solera* derives from the Latin

solum, meaning floor or foundation. While the system of
refreshing one series of casks from a newer series of casks is
described overall as a *solera*, the *solera* itself is, strictly
speaking, only the original series – the foundation from which
the wine is drawn for shipping. All the other rows, or 'scales' as
they are known, are called *criaderas* – nurseries.

The sherry is drawn from the *solera* two or three times a
year. The casks are never emptied; they are topped up with
wine from the first *criadera*, which in turn is replenished from
the second and so forth down the scale to the youngest
criadera, ready to take the freshly classified wines from the
añada. About 15 per cent of the contents of the cask are drawn
off each time. It is always the wine which moves, by siphon,
from *criadera* to *criadera*. The casks stay put – and they
virtually never wear out.

Of white American oak, *bodega* butts are greatly valued. To
be used in the *solera* system, they must first be seasoned – so
as not to impart woody tastes into the wine. The great ranks of
casks, piled up to five rows high (the maximum permitted) in
the Sandeman *bodegas* do not each represent a single *solera*,
and the number of scales is by no means limited to five. The

Oloroso solera in a cathedral-like
bodega.

120

principal Sandeman scale of *oloroso*, for example, consists of 14 *criaderas* leading up to a *solera* which probably dates from the 1850s. All the casks, as far as is known, are the originals.

The number of casks making up a *solera* varies considerably. For basic wines the figure may be more than 1,000. For fine sherry such as Don Fino, the number is just 290 – the *criaderas* being selected, simply by tasting, from Sandeman's main *fino criadera*. As mentioned in the last chapter, the *solera* for a very rare sherry such as Royal Ambrosante consists of a mere 18 casks.

Different storage conditions suit the different styles of wine. The *fino soleras* are all to be found in the main bodegas in Jerez, in the relative cool, and where they can receive the constant supervision they need. These are delicate wines, fortified today to a modest 17.5 per cent alcohol or, in the case of Don Fino (accounting for about a tenth of the *finos* made by Sandeman), only 16.5 per cent. *Amontillado* wines, which begin life as *finos* but gradually darken as the *flor* is allowed to diminish, will stand higher temperatures, but not direct sunlight. Most of these wines are shipped at 17.5 per cent alcohol, though very long-aged examples such as Sandeman's Bone Dry Old Amontillado reach 18.5 per cent, and Royal Esmeralda Rare Amontillado reaches 21 per cent. This is simply due to evaporation over many years, which causes the non-alcoholic elements of the wine to reduce. Canyons of the great blackened butts of *olorosos*, which do not develop a *flor* and gain their great concentration of aroma and flavour, not to mention their deep, dark colour, from slow oxidation, are to be found at several positions on the Jerez site. Sandeman *olorosos* are shipped at between 17.5 per cent alcohol (e.g. Sandeman Character and Armada Cream) and 21 per cent (for Imperial Corregidor).

As a rule, there will be about 75,000 casks in use at the *bodegas*, all of them in or destined for one *solera* or another. By the very complexity of the system, it is easy to lose track of the individual vintages. But of one thing there is no doubt: for sherry to be good it has to mature in the *solera* system. Wines left too long in the *añadas* will ultimately lose all their charm and become dull and lifeless. In making sherry, there is little room for 'vintages of the century'. The vital art is to ensure even working of the scale to maintain the original characteristics of the *solera*. By drawing off controlled quantities and topping up straightaway, the continuity of style is never lost.

Another great part of sherry-making is blending. Most sherries are to a greater or lesser extent blended wines, quite apart from the continuing blending process in the *criaderas*. Sherries commonly consist of three or four wines drawn from different *soleras*, all of the same basic style, but subtly different among themselves. To this blend, PX or *dulce* wines might be added to enrich flavour and aroma. Every blend must then 'marry' for some time, possibly months, to form a homogeneous whole.

The finished wines are ultra-cooled before bottling or

121

shipping in cask or container. This causes the wine to precipitate its natural deposit, and will ensure that it remains brilliant for a considerable time. Like all wines, sherry is very much alive. It is bottled at its prime, and its moment of fulfilment comes as the cork is drawn, and the myriad colours, perfumes and flavours of one of the world's greatest wines unfold.

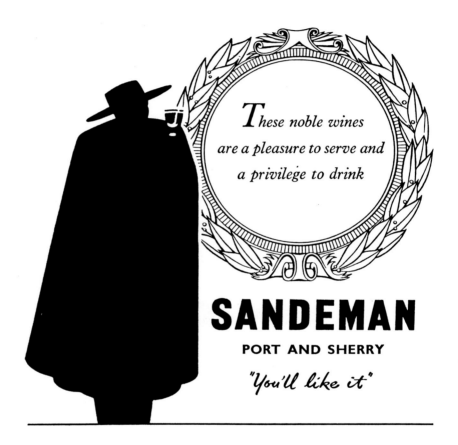
Firing a new sherry butt to temper the wood.

Chapter XI

Sandeman from 1900 – a Chronicle of a Great Mercantile House

Sandeman's house in the Douro is idyllically set on the tip of the promontory at Vale de Mendiz with breathtaking views down the valley. The house is the one furthest to the left in the picture.

In the twentieth century, Sandeman continued in the enterprising tradition that had marked the firm's first 110 years – and in doing so, revolutionised the port and sherry business throughout the world. For these wines, times had changed. They were no longer the exclusive preserve of the British, nor of the moneyed classes. France, Germany, Scandinavia and the United States were becoming major consumers, particularly of port. In Britain, the nation's new, more widespread wealth meant more wine drinkers than ever before, anxious to discover fine wines – but perhaps uncertain *where* to discover them.

But for all the growth of interest in wine, port and sherry had remained comparatively exclusive all the way to the end of the nineteenth century. 'Brand' names were largely unheard of, as these wines were still imported in cask by the merchants for bottling and sale under their own names. Outside the wine trade and a small circle of connoisseurs, the famous port and sherry names of today were quite unknown in 1900.

But Sandeman had already broken the mould. As early as the 1880s, the firm was shipping its wines to London, bottling them in the cellars beneath the St Swithin's Lane headquarters and re-exporting them under the Sandeman label to France. There the wines were advertised to the public and sold in shops just like any other commodity – as would be expected in the world's leading wine-producing nation. Sandeman saw the potential not just in the French market (today the company's largest for port) but in the way wines were marketed there.

The firm began the new century with a clear desire to make itself a name to be reckoned with. In 1900 they had a stand for Porto Sandeman at the Great Paris Exhibition, sending quantities of very fine wines, accompanied by all manner of display materials to illustrate the traditions of the Douro – including exquisitely modelled bullock carts and figures of Portuguese peasants. It was from direct-marketing endeavours such as this that Sandeman soon built up a major re-export trade with France and many other European countries. Soon there were bottling departments at Oporto and Jerez, exporting direct.

In 1902, the old Sandeman partnership was formed into a limited company as Geo. G. Sandeman Sons & Co. Ltd. with Albert George Sandeman, now 69, as Chairman. In 1903, the company appointed its own agent in Ireland, Edward Dillon, to handle sales of branded wines there. At that time, Sandeman accounted for 70 per cent of the Irish market for port. Although

the name was still unknown to most drinkers on the mainland, Sandeman was a household name in Ireland.

Special offers of a type more associated with the present day were common. An enormous advertisement in *The Irish Times* in 1905 was accompanied by a merchant's announcement that a 'sample case' of six Sandeman wines was available at 15s (75p) delivered to the customer's door. Meanwhile, similarly direct advertising was appearing in continental Europe, the United States and in the nations of the British Empire. By 1914, Sandeman were able to announce – in a half-page advertisement in *The Times* – that they had appointed agents in Paris, Berlin, Moscow, Stockholm, New York, Montreal, Sydney, Wellington, Johannesburg and Tientsin.

Sandeman was by far the largest port-shipping business, with property in Vila Nova de Gaia valued, according to a 1906 note in answer to an enquiry from the British consul in Oporto, at £340,000 – an astronomical sum at that time. But the trade had its troubles nonetheless. The British market was plagued with fake wines purporting to be 'port' when in fact hailing from Spain (notably Tarragona) and elsewhere. The Port Wine Shippers' Association, in which Sandeman played a leading role, brought an action against a merchant for selling Tarragona 'port' in 1904 – but it was to be another 20 years before full protection was given to port's name under British law.

In Portugal, the troubles were rather more dramatic. The century began with Oporto closed off from the Douro behind a *cordon sanitaire,* in the grip of a major epidemic. Sandeman's manager, Hugh Ponsonby, took the outbreak to be one of Indian bubonic plague but it turned out to be cholera. The enforcement of the quarantine appears, according to his letters to London, to have been less than rigorous: 'The soldiers of the Cordon are said to be most uncomfortably provided for and they do not keep a very strict watch. Some of our lodge men have contrived without much difficulty to pass to and from their homes as usual.'

In 1909, there came an even more serious disruption to the Oporto trade. Tremendous storms in December swelled the river Douro to 27 metres above its normal level in the valley, causing catastrophic floods in the city. The series of telegrams sent from the Sandeman lodges to London tell the story.

It was the worst flood on record. Sandeman's losses amounted to £35,000. The damage had all been done in three hours in the early morning of 23 December, and took months to repair. Visitors to Sandeman today are still shown the high-water marks reached in the lodges on that night.

Before the great clean-up was complete, another crisis came to the nation in 1910. Years of political violence in Portugal, which had cost the king his life in 1908, finally led to the banishment of his heir, Don Manuel, in the autumn of 1910 and the declaration of a republic. Hugh Ponsonby, writing at harvest time from Sandeman's beautiful house high in the Douro at Vale de Mendiz, reported reflectively to London:

Apparently it is the wish of the people to have a Republic and there is no obvious reason why a people should not choose the form of government they think will suit them. There is no doubt that under the old order there was endless abuse; so it is to be hoped that under the new form of government an end may be put to official jobbery and 'Empenho' (which may be roughly translated as nepotism) and that much greater consideration may be given to the people's wants such as cheaper bread, better roads, sanitation, education, better distribution of taxes etc.

The people of the country are quite accustomed to the idea of a Republic, having the example of Brazil with its wonderful progress before their eyes.

The fighting in Lisbon was very severe. The Guarda Municipal, who are all picked men sworn to loyalty, fought very bravely, but were lowered chiefly by the revolted Artillery and ships in the Tagus: nearly all the Regiments went over to the insurgents. There were probably more deaths from the fighting in Lisbon than will be reported in the Portuguese Press.

Not a shot was fired in Oporto, though at the time there was a fear that if the Regime in Oporto remained loyal there might be a repetition of the Lisbon fighting; but on hearing the result of the Lisbon encounter the Oporto troops caved in at once and the Republic was declared quite peacefully. Not even an hour of work was lost; the men in our Lodges, for instance, continuing quite quietly at their business.

But the progress of the revolution was not to be a smooth one. The hoped-for improvements in the economic life of the country were slow in coming. There were successive counter-revolutions – no less than 20 during the next decade and a half – and serious strikes.

Sandeman in Jerez, meanwhile, had not had a trouble-free start to the century. As a whole, the sherry market was ailing in Britain and in 1901 the wine's reputation suffered what some sections of the Press rather gleefully called a mortal blow. It was the sale by King Edward VII, on his accession, of the very large surplus of sherry that had accumulated in the royal cellars – 60,000 bottles in all. While it seems unlikely the King took such a view, the notion that sherry was *de trop* inevitably spread rapidly in fashionable circles as a result. Certainly the first decade of the century was a discouraging one for sherry in Britain. The trade responded in 1910 by forming the Sherry Shippers' Association of 17 firms, Sandeman included, to promote the wine generically. It was a novel method of promotion, since taken up by many other groups, and still accounts for a large part of sherry advertising activity today.

The Royal Warrant of George V was granted in 1909. The First World War brought great changes to the port and sherry trade in Britain, and not simply because of the obvious interruptions that resulted to the business because of the war. Anglo-Portuguese treaties in 1914 and 1916 finally gave legal

Walter Albert Sandeman, fourth head of the firm, from 1923 to 1937.

The best in the World

SANDEMAN'S PORT

"ONE STAR" 5/-   "PICADOR" 7/6
"THREE STAR" 6/-   "PARTNERS" 9/-

protection to the name port (though it was not until 1923 that this was successfully tested – by Sandeman – in law). During the war, Albert George Sandeman's son Walter Albert ran the company. Albert George, then in his eighties, had effectively retired, and Walter's sons Christopher, Gerard and Patrick were all away at the war for the duration. All three survived and later worked in the company after the war.

The struggle to keep the business going during the war, which inevitably undid much of Sandeman's good work in continental Europe as well as in Britain, was alleviated by a number of happier anecdotes. In 1915, the firm received a postcard from the officers of the 233rd French Infantry Regiment in the trenches at Champagne. Sandeman's port, the message proclaimed, was *'le meilleur des aperitifs devant les Boches'*. In the same year, a British officer in a prisoner-of-war camp at Friedberg, Hessen, sent this cryptic note to a friend in Bristol:

> Will you go to my chemist, John Harvey of Denmark St, and tell him to send me some of his red eye lotion, the prescription of Dr Sandeman in 1908, also some of his green liniment, the prescription of Dr Menthe. One bottle of each may be sufficient. Have these put in a blue poison bottle and labelled pharmaceutically. . .

At a sale to raise funds for the Red Cross in 1918, Sandeman contributed some port with an extraordinary story behind it. The wine had been shipped in 1915, but the vessel was sunk by a German submarine off Milford Haven. One cask, still intact, floated ashore three weeks later at Penzance. The wine was found to be in perfectly good condition, so Sandeman bottled it, and it made up to £5 per case at the sale. Proud purchasers inevitably christened the wine 'shipwreck port'.

It was in 1919 that, as one writer of the day put it, 'The most momentous resolution' was taken by Sandeman. This was to introduce their own proprietary brands at fixed retail prices in Britain. Walter Albert Sandeman explained the thinking behind the policy in a statement to *Harper's Wine & Spirit Gazette* in 1920.

Many of the traditional wine merchants were quick to condemn the move – most of the complaints coming, as Walter Sandeman, drily pointed out, 'from firms who have never done any business with us'. The argument soon spread from the trade press into Fleet Street, with the papers making much of the heated exchanges between Sandeman and other progressive shippers, notably Domecq, and the merchants. The 'Wine Merchants' Union' contributed the following to the debate in 1921:

> In our opinion, if wine merchants stock or recommend the sale of proprietary brands of Ports and Sherries in preference to selling their own wines, etc, bottled under their own labels, they are, in effect, selling their birthright, and it must be purely a question of time before they are relegated to a position no better than that of a distributing cash chemist.

Sandeman

Sandeman's first electric sign high above Piccadilly Circus atop the Café Monico was switched on in 1921 and cost £28 per week, current included. The London *Evening News* was impressed:

> It makes men's throats grow wistful. First the full bottle and the empty glass, then the pouring; the glass is filled to the brim and the bottle disappears. Finally, in letters of a golden hue, you learn the name of the vintner.

In 1925, an analysis of port and sherry imports showed that total sales of the two wines amounted to 45 million litres in Britain – exactly the figure of 50 years previously. But in 1875 the proportion had been 60 per cent sherry and 40 per cent port; now it was 10 per cent sherry and 90 per cent port. The imbalance was about to improve, however, as the fashion for 'sherry parties' (as a genteel alternative to cocktail parties) took hold of the country. The very high port sales of the 1920s and 1930s were largely due to the popularity of 'port and lemon' (ruby port with lemonade) in pubs at the time – a trend that was not to survive the Second World War.

In 1926, Sandeman further consolidated their name as a great shipper of *oloroso* sherries by buying the El Corregidor vineyard at the heart of the Carrascal district. With its four-square house and winery, fortified either for the protection of the original occupant (the *corregidor* is a magistrate-cum-tax-collector) or of the valuable old wines, the estate gives its harvests and its name to today's great Sandeman *olorosos*, Royal Corregidor and Imperial Corregidor.

Press advertisement, 1925.

Above and near right: Classic posters by Jean d'Ylen.

Albert George Sandeman succeeded his
father, George Glas Sandeman, as head
of the firm in 1868, a position he held
until his death in his ninetieth year in
1923. In the meantime he had been
elected a director of the Bank of
England in 1866, served as Governor
from 1895 to 1897, and held numerous
public offices. This caricature is by
'Spy' of *Vanity Fair*, one of the most
celebrated cartoonists of the day.

Sandeman advertising in Britain took a new turn in 1926 with a series of press advertisements drawn by Septimus Scott, featuring 'the partners'. The characters were based on two fictional Sandeman partners, one senior and traditionally minded, the other junior and keenly market-oriented. The copy consisted of dialogues between the two, debating the merits of old and new customs in the wine trade. The advertisements artfully conveyed the message that while Sandeman managers had firm faith in the new commercial methods they had pioneered, they still had the greatest respect for the traditional values of the trade.

The advertisements appeared in the national press, taking the whole of the *Daily Mail*'s front page on two occasions, featuring dialogues such as this exchange on the merits of advertising port:

> *Junior Partner*: 'It is not at all undignified, sir. Advertising is the corollary of the modern business methods.'
> *Senior Partner*: ''Pon my soul, modern business methods seem to me to have little in common with old port!'

Another advertisement dwelt on the quality issue, and drew upon a favourite old saying of George Glas Sandeman, second head of the firm and Walter Sandeman's grandfather:

> *Senior Partner*: 'Your grandfather used to say inferior port never did *him* any harm!'
> *Junior Partner*: 'Great Scott, sir! He really said that?'
> *Senior Partner*: 'He did. And when people like you said "Great Scott!" he would add, with a twinkle in his eye – "You see, it never gets past my nose!"'

It was in October 1928 that Sandeman's world-famous symbol, the Don, made his appearance. There have been numerous colourful tales of how the enigmatic figure became the Sandeman trade mark. They include several versions surrounding a hungry young artist hawking his portfolio, who, taking refuge from the rain, found himself in the portals of 20 St Swithin's Lane and rang the bell on a whim. The facts are a little more prosaic, but it seems right to set the record straight once and for all.

By 1928, Sandeman was well known for its colour posters, one of the earliest of which was based on a painting the firm had bought from a very popular Royal Academy exhibition of works by Septimus Scott. Other posters by leading French artist, Jean d'Ylen, including a rather racy one featuring a leering centaur, had earned for the company a reputation for commissioning innovative work. It was quite normal, therefore, for printers of the day (who then employed their own poster artists) to call upon Sandeman in the hope of doing some business.

French café scene of 1906, by Pierre Brinaud, shows how the Sandeman name was already familiar on the continent years before it was directly advertised in Britain.

Top: Pierrot and partner were recruited to advertise Partners' Port in the 1920s.

The original 'Don' poster by George
Massiot-Brown.

On just such a mission, a representative of the Lochend Printing Co. of Victoria Street, London, called upon Sandeman's Advertising Manager, Eric Marshall-Hardy, in that October of 1928. Marshall-Hardy assured him that he was always interested to see poster and showcard ideas and invited him to submit a design proposal. The task was given to one of the three artists in the Lochend studio, George Massiot-Brown. He produced the figure dressed in stylised Portuguese student's cape and wide-brimmed hat, just like those worn by the *caballeros* of Jerez, silhouetted for dramatic effect, with the sole dash of colour the port in the glass held up for inspection. The background he made yellow-green. Brown, well aware that French poster artists were currently in vogue, signed the artwork G. Massiot – conveniently camouflaging his Scots origins.

Eric Marshall-Hardy was immediately impressed and showed it to Walter Sandeman, who purchased the artwork and all rights in it for 50 guineas (£52.50). The Lochend Printing Co. were later to receive a first order of 1,000 16-sheet colour posters.

The first advertising in which the Don featured appears to have been the national press campaign of 1930. In 1934 the figure was included on the Company's letterheads and on the labels of Apitiv *fino* sherry. Perhaps the first time he was referred to as the Don rather than as the Sandeman was in 1935 when he figured prominently on the label of the newly launched tawny port, Dry Don. The first decanters made as Don figures – now collectors' pieces – had been made by Royal Doulton as early as 1931.

It was in 1933 that America's Prohibition era ended after 14 years. The prospects of restored business with the United States were especially important to Sandeman as they had long been the suppliers to Harveys of Bristol of the popular Bristol Milk and Bristol Cream sherries. In fact, these wines had been finding their way into the United States even during the Prohibition, via buyers in Canada. Sandeman were to continue

The Coronation Don, made by Royal Doulton in 1937.

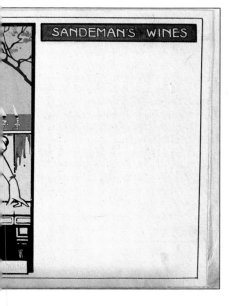

The Silver Don adorns the dining table in the House of Sandeman.

supplying Harveys until after the Second World War, when hugely increased demand for the sherries in the United States reached a level at which Sandeman would no longer meet supplies and the connection was ended.

In Britain, Sandeman had now recruited its own young and enthusiastic sales force to call upon trade customers around the country. Advertising featuring the Don now impressed itself on the British consciousness through such means as the world's largest poster, measuring 9 by 40 metres, seen in London in 1933. A new electric sign featuring the Don was switched on above the Sandeman-owned Queens Head inn, at 52 Piccadilly, in 1938. The previous year, Sandeman had announced that all the 1935 vintage wine was to be bottled by the firm itself. That first entirely Sandeman-bottled vintage, the George V Jubilee wine, was advertised direct at 56s (£2.80) the dozen to the public. 'Perfect uniformity of bottling is secured', Sandeman reminded the merchants, 'which is of such importance to the consumer.'

By now, the wine trade was well accustomed to radical innovations from Sandeman. *The Wine & Spirit Trade Record* acknowledged the beginning of the end of merchant-bottling of vintage ports with a fatalistic comment:

> They certainly have not only 'crossed the Rubicon' and burned their boats, but, as the history of the firm shows, they have been bold in their policy, and although it may not meet with the approbation of many of the other Port shippers it is definitely a step in the direction which the Wine Trade seems to have mapped out for it.

Walter Albert Sandeman, Chairman since 1923, died in 1937. A renowned and highly successful stockbreeder of Aberdeen Angus cattle, his obituary in *The Times* called him 'a typical English country gentleman of the last century' – a kind valediction to the man who had also in his time dragged the British port and sherry trades kicking and screaming into the twentieth century.

Top right: The Sandeman Window Dressing Service (1931) took display materials to wine merchants throughout the country.

He was succeeded by his second son, Gerard, representing the fifth successive generation of the family at the head of the firm. With his younger brother Patrick, Gerard was to administer the diminished affairs of the company in the war years that followed.

As the circular issued by Sandeman to customers at the outbreak of the war in September 1939 put it: 'Until further notice we are unable to guarantee either the execution or price of any order.' Large duty increases were immediately imposed on all wines, and cargoes were lost through enemy action. The company's offices were moved to Marlow in Buckinghamshire, but work and entertaining did continue at St Swithin's Lane. Only relatively minor damage was done to the buildings during the air raids and the vintage ports in the cellars remained undisturbed. When the lack of electric power prevented the movement of the limited number of casks that reached London during that time, the old Capital Crane, installed in 1805, was called up for renewed hoisting duties. It worked perfectly, and continued to do so right up to 1969 when the company moved to other premises.

Right: Poster by Jean d'Ylen (1886–1936), one of the best-known artists of his day. His work was potently persuasive: one of his posters was said to have boosted Brazilian coffee sales in France by 50 per cent in 1926.

Left: Henry Gerard Walter Sandeman, fifth head of the House of Sandeman, from 1937 to 1952.

The 'Don' sign at 20 St Swithin's Lane in 1969, now outside the Sandeman Lodges in Vila Nova de Gaia.

Wine imports into Britain remained restricted until 1949 when, appropriately enough, the electric signs in Piccadilly, the Don included, were switched on again for the first time in a decade. In 1952, the year Sandeman became a public company, Gerard Sandeman retired as Chairman, handing over to Patrick Sandeman, whose sons Timothy Walter and David Patrick were directors of the company. Also in 1952, Sandeman acquired the port shipper Robertson Bros. & Co. Ltd.

It was a time of a sharp fall in port sales in Britain – they dropped a third in six months in 1952 – and Patrick Sandeman relished telling the newspapers that the obvious cause of this temporary blip was the new-fangled trend for men to do the washing-up after meals. 'Nowadays we get straight up from our meals,' he told the *Daily Mail* with a matchingly straight face, 'leave out the port, and get on with the work. Of course *I* don't. I do the washing up and drink the port afterwards.'

Patrick Sandeman was an energetic campaigner for port and sherry as wines for all types of people, and conducted countless tastings around the country to introduce Sandeman to as many people as possible. It gave him particular pleasure, too, to announce in 1955 that Sandeman had opened up a new market for their sherry – namely Spain, with a modest 250 cases for that year. (Today, that figure is more than 40,000.)

Above: Bottling Sandeman 1955 Vintage Port and corking with the boot and flogger at the Dorchester Bond, 1957.

Far left: Patrick Walter Sandeman, sixth head of the firm, from 1952 to 1959.

The company's new Chairman in 1959 was Timothy Walter Sandeman, now the sixth generation of the family to head the firm. He was to preside over a period of great change for the House of Sandeman, which was to begin with the mechanisation of bottling, in 1959; the last vintage to be hand-bottled at St Swithin's Lane was the 1955, carried out by a team headed by craftsman Harry James, complete with boot-and-flogger corking. For the last ten years of tenure in its old City home, Sandeman used the cellars only for limited storage of old vintages.

In 1961 the company bought Sandeman & Sons Ltd of Edinburgh, Scotch whisky blenders and wine and spirit merchants. The two firms had been involved in trade mark disputes back in the 1930s but had previously been unconnected, though apparently the Scottish firm had been founded in 1760 by a cousin of George Sandeman. The company was wound up in the 1970s.

In 1962, Sandeman bought Offley Forrester, the port shippers with whom the Sandeman family had ancient connections, and acquired shares in J.R. Phillips, at that time principally a sherry shipper. This latter interest was sold in 1973.

In 1964, the firm launched Porto Branco white port in a bid to popularise the style that by then accounted for 30 per cent of Sandeman port sales in France. In 1965, the first television commercial for Sandeman was broadcast, on the 'Find the Don' theme. In 1967, Sandeman made their first shipment of sherries to the USSR. The Company had sold wine to Russia in earlier times – but not since the Revolution of 1917. Other sales during 1967 included the Castle & Co. off-licence chain, to Allied Breweries, and 50 per cent of the shares in Offley Forrester to St Raphael (the remaining shares were sold subsequently).

Another point of departure in 1967 was the retirement of Sandeman's most famous *capataz*, or foreman, from the *bodegas* at Jerez. Lorenzo Mesa had started work for the Company in August 1912, aged just ten years old, and only five months after his father had died after many years with the firm. In an interview in 1989, Mesa was still well able to recall his earliest days, when he was first trained by the then resident partner Walter Buck to assess the wines, and undertook the more mundane tasks of the apprentice, such as delivering the daily papers to Christopher Sandeman in the splendid *palacio* across the way from the *bodegas*.

In 1969, Sandeman were on the move. With the ending of the lease on St Swithin's Lane, head office was, with appropriate ceremony, transferred to 37 Albert Embankment, overlooking the Thames opposite the Tate Gallery. On 28 November 1979, the international drinks company Seagram made an agreed offer for the shares of Geo. G. Sandeman Sons & Co. Ltd. Timothy Walter Sandeman remained as the company's Chairman until 1982, when he was succeeded by his younger brother David Patrick, who represented the Sandeman family's continued presence at the head of the company as it embarked on its third century in 1990. In May 1990, his son George was appointed General Manager of Sandeman, Oporto.

The 1980s brought in a new era of rapid expansion for the firm, enabled by its membership of the House of Seagram. During the decade many new wines were launched, starting with one that the founder, George Sandeman, who was such an admirer of Bordeaux wines, would surely have approved of. Sandeman claret, produced by the *négociant* house for which Sandeman had been London agents for so many years, Barton & Guestier, was introduced in 1981. In that year Barton & Guestier, also members of the House of Seagram, once again became distributors for Sandeman in France. Sandeman port sales in France rose from 103,000 cases in 1982 to 240,000 cases in 1989.

In 1982, new developments at the lodges in Vila Nova de Gaia included the inauguration of a high-tech bottling plant capable of filling 12 million bottles a year. With annual sales of around 15 million bottles of port, that capacity has long since been exceeded. It was also in 1982 that Sandeman launched a new brand of port, Founders Reserve. A mature port blended from the wines of vintage years, Founders is very much the flagship for Sandeman in the expanding market for high-quality reserve wines for after-dinner drinking. These were exciting times for the sherry trade in Germany, where Sandeman sales have grown phenomenally: from 101,000 cases in 1977 to 224,000 in 1982 (when Seagram Deutschland took over distribution) to more than 580,000 in 1988.

In 1984, the House of Sandeman moved from its Albert Embankment offices to 17 Dacre Street, opposite New Scotland Yard. Now began an important series of new wine launches. In that year came Character Medium Dry Sherry, a classic pale gold *oloroso* from wines with an average of ten years' maturity, was introduced in the same year.

The familiar Sandeman brand name Apitiv took on a new role in 1985. Formerly the name on Sandeman's great *fino* sherry – since rechristened Don Fino – Apitiv now proclaimed Sandeman's driest and lightest style of white port, a classic aperitif wine for serving chilled. This was followed by an outstanding range of Dry Rare Sherries: Bone Dry Amontillado, with an estimated age of 20 years, Dry Old Palo Cortado, estimated age 30 years, and Dry Old Oloroso, estimated age 22 years. In 1988, Sandeman's award-winning Imperial 20 Year Old Tawny Port was re-joined by Royal 10 Year Old Tawny.

In 1988, too, the House of Sandeman made a major new investment in the Alto Douro by purchasing a major vineyard. Quinta do Vau lies in the prime region of cultivation to the south of the river about five kilometres east of Pinhão. Of the 79 hectares, 12 are planted with old vines, producing about 5,000 cases of vintage-quality port, but the large part of the estate has been entirely replanted – or, by way of a massive excavation programme – brought under vine for the first time.

Quinta do Vau signals the future for viticulture in the Douro. As the vineyards will always be, it is largely terraced, but will be accessible to tractors via the diagonal tracks specially excavated for the purpose. Planting is according to the recommendations made for the area by the Technical Adviser

A view of the Douro valley with Quinta do Vau in the foreground.

to Portugal's Ministry of Agriculture, all Richter 00 root stock as follows: Tinta Roriz 35 per cent, Touriga Nacional 20 per cent, Touriga Francesca 20 per cent, Tinta Barroca 20 per cent, and Tinta Cão 5 per cent. By the year 1995, Quinta do Vau will be producing the fruit for 34,000 cases of high-quality wine annually. It will ensure the supply not just for vintage ports, but for Founders Reserve, Sandeman Late Bottled Vintage, Royal 10 Year Old and Imperial 20 Year Old Tawny Ports – a foundation of great wines, for generations of Sandemans to come.

Chapter XII

Enjoying the Wine

Port

Port is now a truly international wine. And because it is, port is produced to suit a very diverse range of tastes, made for drinking on numerous different occasions. In France, Sandeman's largest port market for more than 25 years, white, ruby and tawny ports are enjoyed as aperitif wines – just as they are in Belgium, Italy and Portugal itself, all three now even larger consumers of Sandeman ports than Great Britain. No longer is port regarded as a 'cold-climate' wine. In the United States, where Sandeman sales have grown rapidly in recent years, the fastest-expanding market is southern California.

So much for a wine that has in the past had its delights obscured by lingering misconceptions about how, when and where to enjoy it. Every different nation in the wide world of port-drinking may have customs of its own, but none can claim any more 'correctness' than any other.

In Portugal, for example, it is common to serve tawny port, slightly chilled, as a drink before lunch or dinner. Likewise, white port is served well chilled, perhaps even with ice and topped up with soda or tonic, complete with a twist of lemon peel. These customs have now been adopted throughout the port-drinking world for white and tawny wines.

Red, or ruby, port is best served at about 15°C (60°F) or, to be a little less precise, at a cool 'room' temperature. The very warm temperatures to which homes are now commonly heated in northern winters, 21°C (70°F) or even higher, are really too high a level at which to serve any kind of wine. The true flavours of a Founder's Reserve or Royal 10 Year Old Tawny would certainly be masked by serving the wine too warm. It makes sense, therefore, not to keep port in a kitchen, near a radiator or fire, or in a warm cupboard.

Today's Sandeman ports, with the sole exception of vintage, are all ready to drink once they have been bottled. Even a venerable wine such as Imperial 20 Year Old Tawny, which does all its maturing in cask, is best enjoyed within a year or two of purchase. Unlike 'table wines', port does not have to be drunk within a day or so of opening the bottle. White, tawny or ruby ports all keep very well in a recorked bottle or in a stoppered decanter for up to several weeks. Again, vintage port is the only exception to this rule.

Decanters are pleasing to use for all kinds of port, but necessary only for vintage wines, as it is only these that have been aged in the bottle rather than the cask, and thus have thrown their deposits in the bottle. Late Bottled Vintage has thrown its deposit in cask, and been filtered before bottling, so normally it does not *need* decanting.

Serving a fine vintage port calls for a few preliminaries that are no mere ritual. Stand the wine upright, taking care not to shake it, so that the deposit settles at the bottom of the bottle. Try to allow at least 12 hours for it to settle fully. Holding the bottle steady, next remove the seal from over the cork and clean away any specks with a damp cloth. Pull the cork, preferably with a Screwpull or two-way corkscrew that enables it to be done without moving the bottle about too much. Again, clean off any specks.

Now all that is needed is a clean decanter and a steady hand. Pour the wine very gradually, keeping an eye on the deposit or 'crust' to see that it does not move beyond the shoulder of the bottle. It is very helpful to place a light or candle behind the bottle to give a better view, but not absolutely necessary.

Another useful aid is a decanting funnel – some makes of which even incorporate a mesh filter to trap any deposit that may find its way past the shoulder. Given a slow, steady pour, little wine should be lost. As a very general rule, the younger a vintage port is, the longer should be the period between decanting and serving the wine. Thus, a Sandeman 1970 could benefit from eight or so hours in the decanter, whereas a great rarity from, say, 1911, which would be adversely affected by more than brief exposure to the air, would be decanted immediately before serving.

'Passing the port' is one of the rituals that cannot claim to be based in purely practical origins. The custom of circulating the port decanter clockwise probably simply arises from the fact that most people are right-handed, but the convention that the decanter must keep moving around the table until it returns to the host is nothing more than a quaint rite much enjoyed in the observance by port shippers and other traditionalists. Simply for the record, the conventions further decree that the host may, before circulating the decanter, pour port for the guests to his (or her) immediate right and left. Gentlemen may pour for the lady to their left. If the decanter is not passed soon enough by a distracted guest, his or her neighbour may issue an oblique, but not direct, plea by making some remark about having a passport renewed or keeping the shine on the table (a reference to the polishing action of moving the port around on its coaster).

These innocent rites of after-dinner drinking afford much pleasure but do not of course materially affect the way the wine tastes. What *does* count in this respect is the type of glass used. A plain uncut glass allows the clearest inspection of the wine's colour and, even more important, a glass of reasonably generous size has room for a good measure without being filled to more than two-thirds full. This enables the drinker to 'nose' the port and relish the infinite complexities of the bouquet. The traditional glasses for port, such as the tulip or barrel-shaped type used in the Sandeman lodges, are ideal for nosing the wine, as they taper slightly to the rim, retaining the aroma.

As for the foods which match port, cheese in general and Stilton in particular have a special affinity. It is worth remembering how well other English cheeses go with port. Plain Farmhouse Cheddar is the perfect complement to port at any time of the day. Other ideal foods include the traditional offerings served at dinners in the Factory House in Oporto – nuts and dried fruits, mostly grown in or close by the Douro vineyards. Fresh almonds and walnuts are particularly delicious with port, as are dried brazils and cobnuts. Among fresh fruits, table grapes are a natural choice, but pears or sweeter fruits such as figs or ripe plums go very well.

The infinite nuances of its colour, bouquet and flavour, the generosity of its fruitiness, satisfy the senses in a comfortably complete way. Shared in good company, port really needs no other partner.

Decanting vintage port is no mere ritual – it is vital to the enjoyment of this greatest of after-dinner wines.

Right: Oloroso sherries such as Armada Cream make a match with many kinds of food.

Far right: The Wednesday Lunch at the Factory House, Oporto.

Pages 140 and 141. Above: Timothy Walter Sandeman, Chairman 1959–1982.

Below: Founders Reserve maturing in cask at the Sandeman lodges.

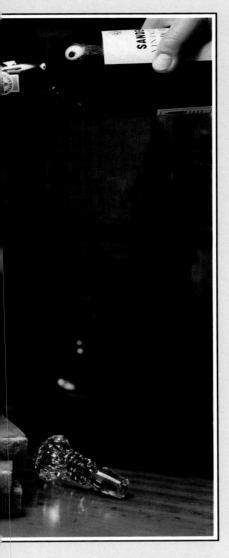

Sherry

Sherry is a white wine which encompasses a truly extraordinary range of flavours. At one end of the scale is the pale, light and sea-breeze-fresh dry sherry epitomised by Sandeman Don Fino. At the far-distant opposite end stands the opulent richness and huge fragrance of a rare *oloroso* such as Royal Corregidor and Imperial Corregidor.

In the heat of Andalusia, they drink *fino*. Chilled so that it beads the *copita* glass with condensation, the wine is enjoyed not merely as an aperitif, but with every kind of food. Mostly, the Spanish take their sherry with *tapas* – 'covers' so-called because a plate was put on top of the sherry glass. *Tapas* bars have now spread from Spain to northern Europe and the United States, vying with each other as they always have in their home country to offer the most delicious little dishes of seafoods, spicy meats, potato and other salads – all foods for which light, dry sherry seems naturally to have been ordained.

Fino sherry is always at its best when treated like a white table wine. Apart from serving it chilled, it needs to be drunk up within a few days of opening, before it loses its freshness. That's why *fino* sherries, Don Fino among them, are widely sold in half bottles as well as full-size bottles. Like all sherries today, the *fino* wines are ready to drink as soon as they have been bottled.

Amontillado and *oloroso* sherries are wines to savour on their own or with a simple snack of nuts or fruit. The fuller 'dessert' sherries such as Sandeman's Armada Cream – a rich *oloroso* – make a sublime accompaniment to puddings, fruit and mild, semi-hard or hard cheeses. As with tawny and ruby ports, the darker sherries can be served slightly cool, and ideally not above 15°C (60°F).

All sherry is naturally dry, whether *fino*, *amontillado* or *oloroso*. The richer versions of these wines, devised centuries ago by means of judicious blending with naturally sweet wines specially prepared from Pedro Ximenes grapes, are the natural

choice for people living in cold climates. But in the major sherry-drinking nations such as Britain, Germany, the Netherlands and the United States there is always a good choice of both styles – and it is essential to read labels to check whether the wine is dry, medium or rich. All Sandeman sherries have explicit back labels describing the wines' particular styles.

The richer wines do have a longer natural life than *finos* once opened, and should stay in good condition for several weeks if kept in a cool place. As with ports, kitchens and warm cupboards are not the best place to keep wines. A cool larder would be ideal, as it will also keep the wines at a good temperature for drinking.

The decanter of sherry that was *de rigueur* in Victorian dining rooms (the wine was commonly served throughout meals at that time) might have been a handsome showpiece, but did not always keep the sherry at its best. Today's wines do not throw a deposit in bottle, and thus do not need decanting for any practical reason. An exception to this rule is Sandeman's range of Rich Rare Sherries. If kept for more than two years or so, these wines may start to throw a deposit in the bottle. This is because the wines have undergone minimum filtration in order to maintain their full character. The answer is to decant the wine, just as with port. Kept stoppered, these venerable sherries will happily stay in prime condition in the decanter for several weeks.

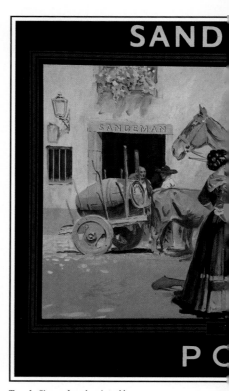

Top: In Sherry Land, painted by Septimus Scott in 1910 and exhibited at the Royal Academy in London, was bought by Sandeman to use for some of the firm's earliest colour advertisements. The wine in the foreground was painted in at a later stage – in the original, a flamenco dancer's hat lay in this position.

Two Centuries of Vintage Port

Sandeman vintage ports date back to the firm's first year, with the 1790, shipped by George Sandeman in 1793. There followed the 1797, described by George Sandeman over a glass with the Duke of Wellington at Torres Vedras in 1809 as 'the finest port wine ever known'. Other early Sandeman vintages included the 1811 'Comet' and 1815 'Waterloo', the 1822 and the 1834. Sandeman's wine in the classic 1847 vintage was tasted by Michael Broadbent in 1956 and recorded in his *Great Vintage Wine Book* as having 'a beautiful autumnal colour; unbelievable on the palate'. Other notable vintage years for Sandeman included 1851, 1858, 1863 and 1868.

The notes on vintages from 1870 that follow are largely from the reports made by Sandeman managers in the Douro at the time of the harvest and as the wine was being made. (The notes were compiled for an epic 1971 tasting of 'One Hundred Years of Sandeman Vintage Port', in which 24 wines were shown.) This is a complete list of vintage ports shipped by Sandeman from 1870 to the present day.

1870 In imperial pints, originally shipped as dry, medium and rich. The vintage at the time of bottling was very fine and had good body.

1872 1873 1875 1878 1880 1881 1884

1887 At the time of the vintage the grapes seemed ripe and in better condition than for some years past. The quantity was less than anticipated but it quickly became clear that this wine was going to be of good quality. This was the 'Queen Victoria's Jubilee' vintage.

1890 1892 1894

1896 This was a rather green vintage as the grapes were not fully ripe when picked and the wines were in consequence a little thin and lacking in colour, although ultimately they developed surprisingly well. Some shippers who did not declare the following vintage were said to have added some of the 1897 wines to their 1896s to remedy the lack of colour.

1897 Like the vintage of exactly a century earlier, a legendary Sandeman wine. The vintage got off to a poor start in bad weather with the first grapes 'very irregular and somewhat dried up so that the early fermentations were too rapid'. But the weather improved, and the latter part of the harvest produced wines with notable colour and flavour. It is an open secret that the Sandeman 1897 was fortified with Scotch whisky due to a brandy shortage.

1900 Vineyards that delayed picking until October made much the best wine, as they avoided the downpours of late September that spoiled the harvest. A very successful Sandeman vintage.

1904 'The bunches of grapes are very numerous, the grapes are very large and every grape is bursting with liquid', reported Hugh Ponsonby from the Alto Douro in late September. A vintage with average colour but great delicacy. Another severe shortage of brandy meant that much of the wine was made with spirit from Hamburg. Sandeman did, however, have adequate brandy stocks and made a normal vintage.

1908 A classic year in the Douro, with a cold winter, warm spring and steady, but not excessive, heat throughout the summer. The new-made wines were 'thick, flavoury, ripe, burnt, with quite the old-style smell of roasted coffee. We would say they will prove quite as good as our 1897 lot.'

1911 Sandeman were the only firm to declare and ship the 'Coronation' (of George V) vintage in significant quantity. The vintage started in October after a spell of very hot weather. The grapes were very ripe and a large part of the harvest had turned to raisins on the vine, on stalks that had become very dry and brown – a condition which can cause excessively high fermentation temperatures. The fruit was therefore stripped off the stalks before pressing, and while the yield from the very shrivelled grapes was only half what would normally be expected, there was great colour and sweetness in the musts. It

---

enabled Sandeman to make an exceptional wine in a difficult year. Ernest Cockburn wrote of the Sandeman 1911 that it 'will long be remembered as a first class specimen of all that is best in Vintage Port'.

1912 A good harvest in fine weather was nine-tenths completed for Sandeman before the rain came. None of the late-picked fruit was included in the vintage port. An outstanding vintage.

1917 It had been a very dry summer and therefore the grapes were rather burnt. Rain at the end of September helped swell the fruit and the wines had good body and richness as well as colour.

1920 After an inauspicious start – April brought rain, hailstorms and frost and June saw a sudden outbreak of mildew – manager Hubert Jennings was able to report from the Alto Douro that 'the soft rains which fell at intervals during the first fortnight of September did nothing but good'. Quantity was short, but quality 'distinctly above the average'.

1924 A small vintage in which much of the harvest was rather underripe.

1927 One of the great wines of the century, from a large harvest picked in perfect conditions. Hubert Jennings wrote on 21 October: 'The wines all have beautiful colour, fair body, and considerable flavour, but are distinctly green in the finish, but we hope this greenness will tend to disappear as the wines get better together – they remind us in many ways of 1912, but they have more flavour.'

1934 Sandeman's first vintage declaration in seven years at first seemed an unlikely candidate after poor weather up to April affected flowering and the setting of the fruit. But as an advertisement for the Sandeman 1934 claimed in 1936: 'It has great flavour and shows exceptional ripeness, the latter feature ensuring early maturity which, nowadays, is so highly desirable.'

1935 By August it looked as if this would be a poor vintage, as the grapes were very backward, due to a cold spring and very dry summer. The rain came just in time and the harvest took place in ideal weather. To mark George V's Jubilee in this year, the Sandeman bottles were specially embossed with a medallion – and a further medallion in honour of the fact that the bottling year, 1937, was that of the Coronation of George VI.

1942 A small vintage of good quality. All Sandeman's wines were bottled in Oporto due to the war.

1945 Drought in 1943 and 1944 continued through the winter of 1945 into a very hot and dry summer. But there were some useful showers in late August and the vintage began soon after – with Sandeman starting later than most on 10 September. The grapes had tough skins with little juice but were very sweet. The wine had exceptional colour and bouquet. This great vintage was offered to the trade in 1947 at £4 a case (about £11

The Sandeman Bicentenary tulip, bred by Konijnenburg & Mark at De Keukenhof in the Netherlands, and 'baptised' on April 24th 1990.

duty paid). Today Sandeman 1945 fetches £1,000 a case at auction, and is still drinking very well.

1947 Vintage started on 22 September after a year of ideal weather. The yield was larger than expected, producing wine of medium colour and good quality, and was predicted – correctly – to mature early into an attractive and delicate port.

1950 A cool summer meant grapes were rather backward and stalks particularly green. But sugar content was about average and the wine of good quality with reasonable colour.

1955 Heavy rains in the preceding autumn and winter were followed by a good summer. Wines had particularly good colour and a higher than average sugar level – although quality did vary noticeably between different areas. The best wines were used to make an exceptional vintage port.

1958 A very hot early autumn after a cold and wet summer produced a better than expected vintage. Reports from the Douro spoke of wines that 'on the whole have good colour and have that attractive pink look of healthy wine'.

1960 'The picking started in brilliantly fine and hot weather, the grapes perfect, probably the finest looking grapes the Douro has seen for a long time', reported manager Gwyn Jennings on 19 September. The vintage turned out correspondingly well, still providing excellent drinking today (provided it has been stored under the right conditions).

1963 By October it was clear that this was destined to be an exceptional year. Gwyn Jennings reported on the 5th that 'The year has run according to the book, though the rain in mid September did give us, most shippers and certainly the farmers, a fright. However all is well. The grapes are in perfect condition.' Sandeman 1963 is deeply coloured, with considerable tannin, now ready for drinking – but set to improve for years to come.

1966 In a mixed vintage, very fine wines were made in some of the best areas of the Alto Douro, although in only relatively small quantities. Drinking very well now.

1967 A year of below average rainfall and only moderate summer heat meant late-ripening fruit and an exceptionally late harvest by Sandeman. The wine was judged to have more colour and quality than the 1966s. A well-balanced port now at its peak.

1970 Heavy rainfall in August was followed by fine, warm weather at vintage time, with picking starting on 24 September. The wines had a very impressive colour, with good fruit. Ready for drinking now, the Sandeman 1970 has not in fact turned out to be quite the classic wine that was expected, but is nevertheless very good.

1975 A good summer followed by rainfall early in September presaged a vintage harvest and picking took place in ideal conditions. In the end, however, 1975 turned out a light year for all shippers. The Sandeman is now fully mature and not a wine to lay down.

1977 Chairman Tim Sandeman offered this assessment of the Sandeman 1977: 'The grapes from the first-class area were in perfect condition when they were picked, in idyllic weather. First-class sweet grapes obviously make first-class wine, but in addition the 1977s have impressive colour and an attractive firmness, which augurs well for a long life in bottle. The fine quality of Sandeman 1977 Vintage Port is unchallengeable and in our opinion this wine, in due course, will compare favourably with the great wines of the century, such as 1945.' A very great wine to drink from the late 1990s.

1980 David Sandeman, who succeeded his brother Tim as Chairman in 1982, made this early assessment of the 1980: 'After a particularly dry summer, picking began in the first-class areas on 22 September, still in fine, dry weather. Features of the wine at vintage time were its clean and fragrant vitality. Owing to its wealth of colour and fruit, together with its roundness in the mouth and its impressive finish, Sandeman 1980 promises to be a wine of considerable character when mature. The 1980 could be compared with the 1960 Vintage and similarly is likely to be ready to drink earlier rather than later.' For drinking from the mid-1990s.

1982 David Sandeman in 1984: 'The Sandeman 1982 will be long remembered for its remarkable depth of colour and its concentrated grapey nose. This is a firm, robust wine reminiscent of the 1966 with the background and stamina to guarantee its development to a distinguished maturity.' To drink from the late 1990s, and for years beyond.

1985 The first widely declared vintage since 1977. Sandeman 1985, a port for drinking from the beginning of the next century, has been extensively reviewed by wine writers. Comments on the wine in its very earliest stages of development have included the 'very deep black colour' noted in *Decanter*, American writer Robert Parker's 'fruitcake sort of aroma' and, in *The Times*, 'Sandeman's superb spicy cinnamon-like wine'.

Bibliography

The author wishes to acknowledge the assistance of the following books of reference in researching and checking this work: *The Factory House at Oporto* by John Delaforce (Christies); *Facts about Port and Madeira* and *Facts about Sherry*, both written and published by Henry Vizetelly; *From Grape to Glass* (Sandeman); *The House of Sandeman; Port Wine* (The Port Wine Institute); *The Sandeman Family of Perth; Sherry* by Julian Jeffs (Faber & Faber); *Sherry* by Rupert Croft-Cooke (Puttnam); *Sherry and Port* by H. Warner Allen (Constable); *They Went to Portugal* by Rose Macaulay (Penguin).

Index